BIBLE
MEMORY
WORD SEARCHES

BARBOUR
PUBLISHING

© 2016 by Barbour Publishing, Inc.

ISBN 978-1-63609-301-7

All scripture quotations are taken from the King James Version of the Bible.

Published by Barbour Publishing, Inc., 1810 Barbour Drive, Uhrichsville, Ohio 44683, www.barbourbooks.com

Our mission is to inspire the world with the life-changing message of the Bible.

Member of the
Evangelical Christian
Publishers Association

Printed in the United States of America.

Welcome to
BIBLE MEMORY WORD SEARCHES!

The Bible tells us that God's Word illuminates our steps (Psalm 119:105) and that it's quick and powerful and sharper than a two-edged sword (Hebrews 4:12). The Bible is inspired by God (2 Timothy 3:16), and it will endure forever (Isaiah 40:8; Matthew 24:35). In this collection of word searches, you'll find a great way to memorize scripture (and it just happens to be a whole lot of fun)!

Each puzzle begins with scriptures that include blanks for several words. Fill in the blanks and then find those words in the search grid. Don't know some of the missing words? Try finding the words in the search grid first. Entries made up of multiple words include a hint so you know you're looking for more than one word—for example, (3w) means the answer is three words, and they'll be found end-to-end in the search grid. Still stumped? Answer keys can be found in the back of the book.

Are you up for the challenge? Get ready for the heavenly encouragement of scripture and the fun of word games!

Thy word have I hid in mine heart,
that I might not sin against thee.
PSALM 119:11

1

CREATION PART 1
GENESIS 1:1-8

In the _ _ _ _ _ _ _ _ _ _ God _ _ _ _ _ _ _ the heaven and the _ _ _ _ _. **2** And the earth was without form, and _ _ _ _; and darkness was upon the face of the _ _ _ _. And the _ _ _ _ _ _ of God moved upon the _ _ _ _ of the waters. **3** And God said, _ _ _ _ _ _ _ _ _ _ _ _ _ _ (4w): and there was light. **4** And God saw the light, that _ _ _ _ _ _ _ _ (3w): and God divided the light from the _ _ _ _ _ _ _ _. **5** And God _ _ _ _ _ _ the light _ _ _, and the darkness he called _ _ _ _ _. And the evening and the _ _ _ _ _ _ _ were the first day. **6** And God said, Let there be a _ _ _ _ _ _ _ _ _ in the midst of the waters, and let it divide the waters from the _ _ _ _ _ _. **7** And God made the firmament, and _ _ _ _ _ _ _ the waters which were under the firmament from the waters which were above the firmament: and _ _ _ _ _ _ _ (3w). **8** And God called the firmament _ _ _ _ _ _. And the _ _ _ _ _ _ _ and the morning were the _ _ _ _ _ _ _ _ _ (2w).

```
G Y I T R D O O G S A W T I T
W E H C O R I E T P I O H T D
B F A O E Y T O C I T N G W B
D A Y N I G H T V R I E I A N
E V E N I N G U B I O C L S S
H Y O S T I T G N T U A E S A
A A I N G N I N N I G E B O T
L D H O L R O K G O C G E E S
X D L E N O Q B D A R N R I S
T N E M A M R I F W E E E M E
N O N E A V V B D K A K H A N
E C A I W I E E L R T G T N K
R E W O D N Y N T O E N T S R
G S R E T A W H N Y D E E P A
Q E D U O Y N H E C A L L E D
```

2

CREATION PART 2
GENESIS 1:9-19

And God said, Let the waters under the _ _ _ _ _ _ be gathered together unto one place, and let the _ _ _ _ _ _ _ (2w) appear: and it was so. **10** And God called the dry land _ _ _ _ _; and the gathering together of the waters called he _ _ _ _: and God saw that it was good. **11** And God said, Let the earth bring forth grass, the herb yielding seed, and the _ _ _ _ _ _ _ _ _ (2w) yielding fruit after his kind, whose seed is in itself, upon the earth: and _ _ _ _ _ _ _ (3w). **12** And the earth _ _ _ _ _ _ _ _ _ _ _ _ (2w) grass, and herb yielding seed after his kind, and the tree _ _ _ _ _ _ _ _ fruit, whose _ _ _ _ was in itself, after _ _ _ _ _ _ _ (2w): and God saw that it was good. **13** And the _ _ _ _ _ _ _ and the morning were the third day. **14** And God said, _ _ _ _ _ _ _ _ _ _ _ (3w) lights in the firmament of the heaven to divide the day from the _ _ _ _ _; and let them be for signs, and for _ _ _ _ _ _ _, and for days, and years: **15** And let them be for lights in the firmament of the heaven to give light upon the earth: and it was so. **16** And God made two great lights; the greater light to _ _ _ _ _ _ _ _ _ _ (3w), and the lesser _ _ _ _ _ _ to rule the night: he made the _ _ _ _ _ _ also. **17** And God set them in the firmament of the heaven to give light upon the earth, **18** And to rule over the day and over the night, and to divide the light from the _ _ _ _ _ _ _ _: and God saw that it was good. **19** And the evening and the morning were the _ _ _ _ _ _ day.

```
S Y M I A S E A S O N S F D E
E U M O O D T I O N P S I T A
N T I A K G N I N E V E L A L
O E N W T H E A V E N N I O T
R N I E R S B K L T N K N E L
H L H L S A E S S Y A R U Y N
F R U I T T R E E C R A A I C
O H R T A Q E Q U A V D G E K
U A E W R U H T R A E H T L S
R T Y A S O T S I H T W E D E
T C B S R R T L T L S E S I E
H A K S E B E E H I S K I N D
B E E O O L L D O G Y J U G D
L H T M N U M I N H N T N E M
L G A B R O U G H T F O R T H
```

3

CREATION PART 3
GENESIS 1:20-25

And _ _ _ _ _ _ _ (2w), Let the waters bring forth abundantly the moving creature that hath _ _ _ _, and _ _ _ _ that may fly above the _ _ _ _ _ in the open firmament of _ _ _ _ _ _. **21** And God created great _ _ _ _ _ _, and every living creature that moveth, which the _ _ _ _ _ _ brought forth _ _ _ _ _ _ _ _ _ _, after their kind, and every _ _ _ _ _ _ fowl after his kind: and God saw that it was good. **22** And God _ _ _ _ _ _ _ them, saying, Be fruitful, and _ _ _ _ _ _ _ _, and _ _ _ _ _ _ _ _ _ _ _ _ _ (3w) in the seas, and let fowl multiply in the earth. **23** And the evening and the _ _ _ _ _ _ _ were the fifth _ _ _. **24** And God said, Let the earth bring forth the _ _ _ _ _ _ _ _ _ _ _ _ _ _ _ (2w) after his kind, cattle, and creeping thing, and beast of the earth after his kind: and it was so. **25** And God made the _ _ _ _ _ of the earth after his kind, and _ _ _ _ _ _ after their kind, and every thing that _ _ _ _ _ _ _ _ upon the earth _ _ _ _ _ _ _ _ _ _ _ _ (3w): and God saw that _ _ _ _ _ _ _ _ _ (3w).

```
A N C N A L D I A S D O G S A
B L E S S E D D O B M K E E N
U Y O Y G Y L E N W A T E R S
N H A N L N E V A E H N S U O
D N I K S I H R E T F A T T M
A W O I T W A S G O O D L A A
N M G B N X E H K L T Y A E W
T U F I L L T H E W A T E R S
L L Y V C R N H E O L K H C Y
Y T R E A R S T O F O T W G I
W I H E T A H T M O R N I N G
R P G H T R S E F R W E C I R
V L K L L A A I R S O N F V A
D Y A D E H R M E P U Q K I Z
N I N B D C R E E P E T H L L
```

CREATION PART 4
GENESIS 1:26-29, 31; 2:1-3

And God said, Let us make man in our _ _ _ _ _, after our likeness: and let them have _ _ _ _ _ _ _ _ over the fish _ _ _ _ _ _ _ _ (3w), and over the fowl _ _ _ _ _ _ _ _ (3w), and over the _ _ _ _ _ _, and over all the earth, and over every creeping thing that _ _ _ _ _ _ _ _ upon the _ _ _ _ _. **27** So God created man in his own image, in the _ _ _ _ _ _ _ _ _ _ (3w) created he him; male and female _ _ _ _ _ _ _ he them. **28** And God blessed them, and God said unto them, Be _ _ _ _ _ _ _ _ _, and multiply, and _ _ _ _ _ _ _ _ _ _ the earth, and subdue it: and have dominion over the _ _ _ _ of the sea, and over the fowl of the air, and over every living thing that moveth upon the earth. **29** And God said, Behold, I have given you every herb bearing _ _ _ _, which is upon the face of all the earth, and every tree, in the which is the _ _ _ _ _ of a tree yielding seed; to you it shall be for meat. . . . **31** And God saw every thing that he had made, and, behold, it was very good. And the _ _ _ _ _ _ _ and the morning were the _ _ _ _ _ day. . . . **1** Thus the _ _ _ _ _ _ _ and the earth were finished, and all the host of them. **2** And on the _ _ _ _ _ _ _ day God ended his work which he had made; and he _ _ _ _ _ _ on the seventh day from all his work which he had made. **3** And God blessed the seventh day, and _ _ _ _ _ _ _ _ _ _ it: because that in it he had rested from all his work which God created and made.

```
S N I Q S E U E L T T A C E P
C R S E H S I N E L P E R E D
R I A L T S I H T X I S E C I
N A E N O N F T F L E E E N S
O F T O G E I F C V E H P L S
I L L I N V S E E D W T E I A
N D T S I A G N O A T F T A N
I E B L N E T G E E N O H A C
M T U L E H F R U I T F U L T
O S Q Y V O O E V E S T W E I
D E T A E R C O G U L H S I F
I R S G A N O P R A D E I G I
H E A R T H D A L T M A A B E
V M I E S T S N R N E I D T D
I A N C L C A L T I U R F H S
```

5

ADAM
GENESIS 2:7-17

And the LORD God _ _ _ _ _ _ man of the dust of the ground, and breathed into his _ _ _ _ _ _ _ _ the breath of life; and man became a _ _ _ _ _ _ _ _ _ _ (2w). **8** And the LORD God planted a garden eastward in _ _ _ _; and there he put the man whom he had formed. **9** And out of the ground made the LORD God to grow every tree that is pleasant to the sight, and good for food; the _ _ _ _ _ _ _ _ _ _ (3w) also in the midst of the garden, and the tree of _ _ _ _ _ _ _ _ _ _ of good and evil. **10** And a _ _ _ _ _ went out of Eden to water the garden; and from thence it was parted, and became into _ _ _ _ _ _ _ _ _ (2w). **11** The name of the first is _ _ _ _ _: that is it which compasseth the whole land of _ _ _ _ _ _ _, where there is gold; **12** And the gold of that land is good: there is bdellium and the onyx stone. **13** And the name of the second river is _ _ _ _ _: the same is it that compasseth the whole land of Ethiopia. **14** And the name of the third river is _ _ _ _ _ _ _ _: that is it which goeth toward the east of Assyria. And the fourth river is _ _ _ _ _ _ _ _ _. **15** And the LORD God took the man, and put him into the _ _ _ _ _ _ of Eden to dress it and to keep it. **16** And the LORD God _ _ _ _ _ _ _ _ _ _ the man, saying, Of every tree of the garden thou mayest freely _ _ _: **17** But of the tree of the knowledge of _ _ _ _ and _ _ _ _, thou shalt not eat of it: for in the day that thou eatest thereof thou shalt surely _ _ _.

```
L E K E D D I H A V I L A H E
I T U Q S T I E I T E R E E U
V B K R A D O O G H A I E P P
I I N O S I P A Z E T A D F H
N M O R E T R N F O R M E D R
G B W G F D A I K B T A N E A
S E L O E Y L Y C W F I N D T
O D E N G F E G I H O N L N E
U S D W O W I C E E U C C A S
L E G E D S H T H L R I A M T
P R E I V E T T O E H E M M S
O R S A E F H R I V E R E O S
T D F B A D B L I I A H L C A
A R T Y N T F L N L D K E I L
D O E E W A Y N T O S I N H E
```

6

EVE
GENESIS 2:18-25

And the LORD God said, It is not good that the man should _ _ _ _ _ _ _ (2w); I will make him an help meet for him. **19** And out of the ground the _ _ _ _ God formed every beast of the _ _ _ _ _, and every _ _ _ _ of the air; and brought them unto _ _ _ _ to see what he would call them: and whatsoever Adam called every living _ _ _ _ _ _ _ _, that was the name thereof. **20** And Adam gave names to all _ _ _ _ _ _, and to the fowl of the air, and to every beast of the field; but for Adam there was not found an _ _ _ _ _ _ _ _ (2w) for him. **21** And the LORD God caused a deep _ _ _ _ _ to fall upon Adam, and he slept: and he took _ _ _ _ _ _ _ _ _ _ _ (4w), and closed up the flesh instead thereof; **22** And the rib, which the LORD God had taken from man, made he a woman, and _ _ _ _ _ _ _ her unto the man. **23** And Adam said, This is now bone of my _ _ _ _ _, and flesh of my _ _ _ _ _: she shall be called _ _ _ _ _, because she was taken out of Man. **24** Therefore shall a man leave his _ _ _ _ _ _ and his _ _ _ _ _ _, and shall cleave unto his _ _ _ _: and they shall be _ _ _ _ _ _ _ _ (2w). **25** And they were both _ _ _ _ _, the man and his wife, and were not _ _ _ _ _ _ _.

```
D H S E L F E N O O W I P R T
G O Q U D A S D N M L R E B H
O P T E E M P L E H T O C H M
A L L Y K E D E O T S N P A O
P E W O A N N O F N N E G M T
A Y O D N O G L H I E X L H H
S M F G L E U R I L H S G F E
H R I A N Y A W S H U U R U R
A I E R U T A E R C O A E S N
M B L W M F H A I R T G B N I
E F D O U N A Y B O N E S L E
D O N M R A R T S H T I F P P
A S G A O D A E H W L T C I R
L R C N C A T T L E Y P K A W
Z O P T N M R A I F R H L L E
```

THE TEMPTATION OF EVE
GENESIS 3:1-8

Now the serpent was more subtil than any _ _ _ _ _ of the field which the LORD God had made. And he said unto the _ _ _ _ _ _, Yea, hath God said, Ye shall not eat of every tree of the _ _ _ _ _ _? **2** And the woman said unto the _ _ _ _ _ _ _, We may eat of the _ _ _ _ _ _ _ _ _ _ _ _ _ (4w) of the garden: **3** But of the fruit of the tree which is in the midst of the garden, God hath said, _ _ _ _ _ _ _ _ _ _ _ _ (4w) of it, neither shall ye _ _ _ _ _ _ it, lest ye die. **4** And the serpent said unto the woman, Ye shall not _ _ _ _ _ _ _ _ _ _ (2w): **5** For God doth know that in the day ye eat thereof, then your eyes shall be _ _ _ _ _ _, and ye shall be as gods, knowing _ _ _ _ and _ _ _ _. **6** And when the woman saw that the tree was good for food, and that it was _ _ _ _ _ _ _ _ to the eyes, and a tree to be desired to make one _ _ _ _, she took of the fruit thereof, and did eat, and gave also unto her _ _ _ _ _ _ _ with her; and he did eat. **7** And the _ _ _ _ of them both were opened, and they knew that they were _ _ _ _ _; and they sewed _ _ _ _ _ _ _ _ _ (2w) together, and made themselves aprons. **8** And they heard the voice of the LORD God walking in the garden in the _ _ _ _ _ _ _ _ _ _ _ _ (4w): and Adam and his wife hid themselves from the _ _ _ _ _ _ _ _ _ of the _ _ _ _ _ _ _ (2w) amongst the trees of the garden.

```
N T Y A D E H T F O L O O C A
G R O I Q U L O R D G O D S D
N B T S E R P E N T U L B E M
P K B H B B E O S A R W N V R
L A I E N G N C I E D E K A N
E L E D A S R P R T P K E E P
A T P R W S U T G O M A S L R
S Y D T O P T R C N D O O G E
A E R N M C L A E L L X S I S
N Y V C A R W W T L R T M F E
T E H I N B I Y O A Y K T C N
B S A H L E S B U H L D K N C
A N I W U Q E U C S L I I N E
F R U I T O F T H E T R E E S
B O S E M N O Z A Y G O N A N
```

8

NOAH AND THE ARK
GENESIS 6:13-22

And God said unto _ _ _ _, The end of all flesh is come before me; for the earth is filled with _ _ _ _ _ _ _ _ through them; and, behold, I will _ _ _ _ _ _ _ them with the earth. **14** Make thee an ark of _ _ _ _ _ _ _ _ _ _ (2w); rooms shalt thou make in the ark, and shalt pitch it within and without with pitch. **15** And this is the fashion which thou shalt make it of: The _ _ _ _ _ _ of the ark shall be three hundred cubits, the _ _ _ _ _ _ _ of it fifty _ _ _ _ _ _, and the _ _ _ _ _ _ of it thirty cubits. **16** A window shalt thou make to the ark, and in a cubit shalt thou finish it above; and the door of the ark shalt thou set in the side thereof; with lower, second, and _ _ _ _ _ stories shalt thou make it. **17** And, behold, I, even I, do bring a _ _ _ _ _ of waters upon the earth, to destroy all flesh, wherein is the _ _ _ _ _ _ _ _ _ _ _ _ (3w), from under heaven; and every thing that is in the earth _ _ _ _ _ _ _ _ (2w). **18** But with thee will I establish my _ _ _ _ _ _ _ _ _; and thou shalt come into the _ _ _ , thou, and thy sons, and thy wife, and thy sons' wives with thee. **19** And of every _ _ _ _ _ _ _ _ _ _ _ (2w) of all flesh, _ _ _ _ _ _ _ _ _ _ _ _ _ _ (4w) shalt thou bring into the ark, to keep them alive with thee; they shall be male and _ _ _ _ _ _. **20** Of fowls after their kind, and of cattle after their kind, of every creeping thing of the earth after his kind, two of every sort shall come unto thee, to _ _ _ _ _ _ _ _ _ _ _ _ (3w). **21** And take thou unto thee of all food that is eaten, and thou shalt gather it to thee; and it shall be for food for thee, and for them. **22** Thus did Noah; according to all that God _ _ _ _ _ _ _ _ _ _ him, so did he.

```
T N A N E V O C E D Y M G P M
W I L E I D L L A H S C K E D
O E I A W L K B R E A D T H A
O V V D S B I T J N O D D T R
F I I E A R U K B O U H A G V
E L N D B E R T W A R E C N I
V A G N L A S R H H T I H E N
E M T A I T E T T N J G T L W
R E H M D H H W O I C H X W R
Y H I M P O P C U B I T S D O
S T N O N F H E M R K E A G I
O P G C F L O O D E S T R O Y
R E W L U I T Z P U N L E A S
T E D S Q F E M A L E B C E O
A K A H L E C N E L O I V M C
```

9

THE PROMISE
GENESIS 8:1, 15-22

And God remembered _ _ _ _, and every living thing, and all the cattle that was with him in the ark. . . . **15** And God _ _ _ _ _ unto Noah, saying, **16** Go forth of the ark, thou, and thy wife, and thy sons, and thy sons' wives with thee. **17** Bring forth with thee every living thing that is with thee, of all flesh, both of fowl, and of cattle, and of every creeping thing that _ _ _ _ _ _ _ _ upon the earth; that they may _ _ _ _ _ abundantly in the earth, and be fruitful, and _ _ _ _ _ _ _ _ upon the _ _ _ _ _. **18** And Noah went forth, and his _ _ _ _, and his _ _ _ _, and his sons' wives with him: **19** Every beast, every creeping thing, and every fowl, and whatsoever creepeth upon the earth, after their kinds, went forth _ _ _ _ _ _ _ _ _ _ _ _ (4w). **20** And Noah builded an _ _ _ _ _ unto the LORD; and took of every clean beast, and of every clean fowl, and offered _ _ _ _ _ _ _ _ _ _ _ _ _ (2w) on the altar. **21** And the LORD smelled a _ _ _ _ _ _ _ _ _ _ (2w); and the LORD said in his heart, I will not again _ _ _ _ _ the ground any more for man's sake; for the _ _ _ _ _ _ _ _ _ _ _ of man's heart is evil from his _ _ _ _ _; neither will I again _ _ _ _ _ any more every thing living, as I have done. **22** While the earth remaineth, seedtime and _ _ _ _ _ _ _ _, and cold and _ _ _ _, and summer and _ _ _ _ _ _, and day and _ _ _ _ _ _ shall not cease.

```
L O O E S R U C R O U L S T U
O D G S N O A H O W A L T A R
V M H D O I T O K F I R K B E
M A N T S E V R A H N I W K T
U C R H R Q U J Y D E R R S N
L E A G A A K G N I A A S E I
T K T I Z P E K D S E G T V W
I A S N Y P W O T H C D E I B
P P R U O V A S T E E W S N G
L S G N I R E F F O T N R U B
Y M P H H A O O R B O L W W R
O I N O I T A N I G A M I D E
R T H T U O Y E E C H R F C E
R E S O H T E P E E R C E N D
B X S N I R P T Z O M Y S X O
```

GOD'S COVENANT WITH ABRAM
GENESIS 12:1-3; 15:18-21

Now the LORD had said unto _ _ _ _ _, Get thee out of thy _ _ _ _ _ _ _, and from thy kindred, and from thy father's _ _ _ _ _, unto a land that I will shew thee: **2** And I will make of thee a great _ _ _ _ _ _, and I will _ _ _ _ _ thee, and make thy name _ _ _ _ _; and thou shalt be a blessing: **3** And I will bless them that bless thee, and _ _ _ _ _ him that _ _ _ _ _ _ _ thee: and in thee shall all _ _ _ _ _ _ _ _ of the earth be blessed. . . . **18** In the same day the _ _ _ _ made a _ _ _ _ _ _ _ _ with Abram, saying, Unto thy seed have I given this _ _ _ _, from the river of Egypt unto the great river, the river _ _ _ _ _ _ _ _ _: **19** The _ _ _ _ _ _ _, and the _ _ _ _ _ _ _ _ _ _, and the Kadmonites, **20** And the _ _ _ _ _ _ _ _, and the _ _ _ _ _ _ _ _ _ _ _, and the _ _ _ _ _ _ _ _, **21** And the _ _ _ _ _ _ _ _, and the Canaanites, and the Girgashites, and the _ _ _ _ _ _ _ _ _.

```
H E O M N L F A M I L I E S M
S L M A C L O I S E T I N E K
R L D R I B R M E X E K T T Z
E E T B S H B W T P S S T I Z
P C H A S L K E A L Y A R S E
H Z I O E D N S R O A E T U S
A Z V S T R D O H R G N R B C
I T S D I B G Z P D A I D E O
M D E P Z G E Z U N M U S J U
S E T I Z Z I N E K O B E N N
R H I S I A H V D J R I S E T
O I T T R L O C H E I F U S R
H G T C E C G O N A T I O N Y
C R I K P Z D M A S E T H S L
M W H T E S R U C B S T G H S
```

11

ABRAHAM AND ISAAC
GENESIS 22:1-2, 6-13

And it _ _ _ _ _ _ _ _ _ _ (3w) after these things, that God did tempt Abraham, and said unto him, Abraham: and he said, Behold, here I am. **2** And he said, Take now thy son, thine only son _ _ _ _ _, whom thou _ _ _ _ _ _, and get thee into the land of _ _ _ _ _ _; and offer him there for a burnt offering upon one of the _ _ _ _ _ _ _ _ _ which I will tell thee of. . . . **6** And _ _ _ _ _ _ _ took the wood of the _ _ _ _ _ _ _ _ _ _ _ _ (2w), and laid it upon Isaac his son; and he took the fire in his hand, and a knife; and they went both of them together. **7** And Isaac spake unto Abraham his father, and said, _ _ _ _ _ _ _ _: and he said, Here am I, my son. And he said, Behold the fire and the _ _ _ _: but where is the _ _ _ _ for a burnt offering? **8** And Abraham said, My son, God will _ _ _ _ _ _ _ himself a lamb for a burnt offering: so they went both of them _ _ _ _ _ _ _ _. **9** And they came to the place which God had told him of; and Abraham built an _ _ _ _ _ there, and laid the wood in order, and bound Isaac his son, and laid him on the altar upon the wood. **10** And Abraham stretched forth his hand, and took the _ _ _ _ _ to slay his son. **11** And the _ _ _ _ _ _ _ _ _ _ _ _ _ _ (4w) called unto him out of _ _ _ _ _ _ _, and said, Abraham, Abraham: and he said, Here am I. **12** And he said, Lay not thine hand upon the lad, neither do thou any thing unto him: for now I know that thou _ _ _ _ _ _ _ _ God, seeing thou hast not withheld thy son, thine only son from me. **13** And Abraham lifted up his _ _ _ _ _, and looked,

```
M O D K O L C O Q U S M S O R
A N G E L O F T H E L O R D A
H E C M I V W O O D Y R A S G
A V F O N E A G F H M I M D N
R A S E S S T E T A T A L L I
B E M N C T A T N E K H O O R
A H O V A R C H Y B K P J U E
I S U L E E O E S A M C A D F
R V N S E H S R R L C T I N F
E F T Q N T K A E T E V S H O
A S A U C A N B M A O P A K T
R T I A T F I W S R S T A C N
S E N P P Y F K P C R A C N R
X T S C A M E T O P A S S C U
N I C D N O A P H I N L A M B
```

and behold behind him a ram caught in a _ _ _ _ _ _ _ _ by his horns: and Abraham went and took the _ _ _, and offered him up for a burnt offering in the stead of his son.

JACOB AND ESAU
GENESIS 25:21-34

And Isaac intreated the LORD for his wife, because she was _ _ _ _ _ _: and the LORD was _ _ _ _ _ _ _ _ _ of him, and Rebekah his wife conceived. **22** And the children _ _ _ _ _ _ _ _ _ together within her; and she said, If it be so, why am I thus? And she went to enquire of the LORD. **23** And the LORD said unto her, _ _ _ _ _ _ _ _ _ _ (2w) are in thy womb, and two manner of people shall be separated from thy _ _ _ _ _ _; and the one people shall be stronger than the other people; and the elder shall serve the _ _ _ _ _ _ _. **24** And when her days to be delivered were fulfilled, behold, there were _ _ _ _ _ in her womb. **25** And the first came out red, all over like an _ _ _ _ _ _ _ _ _ _ _ (2w); and they called his name _ _ _ _. **26** And after that came his brother out, and his hand took hold on Esau's _ _ _ _; and his name was called _ _ _ _: and Isaac was _ _ _ _ _ _ _ _ _ _ years old when she bare them. **27** And the boys grew: and Esau was a cunning _ _ _ _ _ _ _, a man of the field; and Jacob was a plain man, dwelling in _ _ _ _ _. **28** And Isaac loved Esau, because he did eat of his _ _ _ _ _ _ _: but _ _ _ _ _ _ _ _ loved Jacob. **29** And Jacob sod pottage: and Esau came from the field, and he was faint: **30** And Esau said to Jacob, _ _ _ _ _ _ (2w), I pray thee, with that same red pottage; for I am _ _ _ _ _: therefore was his name called Edom. **31** And Jacob said, Sell me this day thy _ _ _ _ _ _ _ _ _ _ . **32** And Esau said, Behold, I am at the point to die: and what _ _ _ _ _ _ _ shall this birthright do to me? **33** And Jacob said, Swear to me this day;

```
S W O B S N O I T A N O W T C
E D T O E I N T R E A T E D H
S R I W C I S P R O K O R A T
E C F E E D M E X E O B H L H
L D O L D M G R N L L A T A E
I E R S I N Y O A B K R I E E
T S P L U D S C I E B R D J L
N P A O F I O S B U Y E N H B
E I Y H N L S E S G O N T T N
L S E E C P R E A T F D D Z H
J E V F S P O R P H N I U C I
A D T A A A M H U N T E R K L
C N E I I E U T S N I W T M S
O B R N N H S T R U G G L E D
B I R T H R I G H T P H C A T
```

and he sware unto him: and he sold his birthright unto Jacob. **34** Then Jacob gave Esau bread and pottage of _ _ _ _ _ _ _ _; and he did eat and drink, and rose up, and went his way: thus Esau _ _ _ _ _ _ _ _ his birthright.

13

MOSES IN THE BASKET
EXODUS 2:1-10

And there went a man of the _ _ _ _ _ _ _ _ _ _ _ _ (3w), and took to wife a daughter of Levi. **2** And the woman conceived, and _ _ _ _ _ _ _ _ (3w): and when she saw him that he was a _ _ _ _ _ _ child, she hid him _ _ _ _ _ _ _ _ _ _ (2w). **3** And when she could not longer hide him, she took for him an ark of _ _ _ _ _ _ _ _ _, and daubed it with slime and with _ _ _ _ _, and put the child therein; and she laid it in the flags by the river's brink. **4** And his _ _ _ _ _ _ stood afar off, to wit what would be done to him. **5** And the daughter of _ _ _ _ _ _ _ came down to _ _ _ _ _ _ _ _ _ _ (2w) at the river; and her maidens walked along by the river's side; and when she saw the ark among the flags, she sent her _ _ _ _ to fetch it. **6** And when she had opened it, she saw the _ _ _ _ _: and, behold, the babe wept. And she had _ _ _ _ _ _ _ _ _ _ on him, and said, This is one of the Hebrews' _ _ _ _ _ _ _ _ _. **7** Then said his sister to Pharaoh's _ _ _ _ _ _ _ _ _, Shall I go and call to thee a nurse of the _ _ _ _ _ _ women, that she may nurse the child for thee? **8** And Pharaoh's daughter said to her, Go. And the maid went and called the child's mother. **9** And Pharaoh's daughter said unto her, Take this child away, and nurse it for me, and I will give thee _ _ _ _ _ _ _ _ (2w). And the women took the child, and _ _ _ _ _ _ _ _ _ (2w). **10** And the child _ _ _ _, and she brought him unto Pharaoh's daughter, and he _ _ _ _ _ _ _ _ _ _ _ _ _ (3w). And she called his name _ _ _ _ _: and she said, Because I _ _ _ _ _ _ _ _ (2w) out of the water.

```
I H O U S E O F L E V I C S O
O D W G F L E S R E H H H S A W
D H R R A S T D Y H P A C O R
G T I E T N M L W E C O H S P
M I H W E R D I T S M Q I C H
A D C M R O E H E P U S L D E
I E T A O L L C A S T N D A T
D S I G W E A S C E O Y R U G
C R P A E R S J R S A T E G W
E U H Y U I P H A C K I N H E
S N A Q O L S E G A W Y H T R
E I R N O S R E H E M A C E B
S G A B O A D Z F F Y N S R E
O H O N B U L R U S H E S M H
M T H R E E M O N T H S D O X
```

14

MOSES AND THE BURNING BUSH
EXODUS 3:1–8

Now Moses kept the flock of Jethro his _ _ _ _ _ _ _ _ _ _ _ (3w), the priest of _ _ _ _ _ _: and he led the _ _ _ _ _ to the backside of the desert, and came to the _ _ _ _ _ _ _ _ _ of God, even to Horeb. **2** And the _ _ _ _ _ _ _ _ _ _ _ _ _ _ (4w) appeared unto him in a flame of fire out of the midst of a _ _ _ _: and he looked, and, behold, the bush burned with _ _ _ _, and the bush was not _ _ _ _ _ _ _ _. **3** And _ _ _ _ _ said, I will now turn aside, and see this great sight, why the bush is not burnt. **4** And when the LORD saw that he turned aside to see, God called unto him out of the midst of the bush, and said, Moses, Moses. And he said, Here am I. **5** And he said, Draw not nigh hither: put off thy _ _ _ _ _ from off thy feet, for the place whereon thou standest is _ _ _ _ _ _ _ _ _ _ (2w). **6** Moreover he said, I am the God of thy father, the God of _ _ _ _ _ _ _, the God of _ _ _ _ _, and the God of _ _ _ _ _. And Moses hid his _ _ _ _; for he was afraid to look upon God. **7** And the LORD said, I have surely seen the _ _ _ _ _ _ _ _ _ _ _ of my people which are in _ _ _ _ _, and have heard their cry by reason of their taskmasters; for I know their _ _ _ _ _ _ _; **8** And I am come down to deliver them out of the hand of the Egyptians, and to bring them up out of that land unto a good land and a large, unto a land flowing with _ _ _ _ _ _ _ _ _ _ _ _ (3w); unto the place of the _ _ _ _ _ _ _ _ _ _, and the Hittites, and the Amorites, and the Perizzites, and the Hivites, and the Jebusites.

```
S O R B O U B M O U N T A I N
P K A S D C U A L T L U R A O
T C E A T U S L M I D I A N I
A O F F A T H E R I N L A W T
C N O I L E E T S M U E O R C
A S S S H O E S P H O Y R K I
N U W T H E C S N Y R W O I L
A M O S E S C K E L G E C A F
A E R N A Q U H S L Y E E W F
N D R O L E H T F O L E G N A
I B O G G D A J B B O W X A B
T C S M I L K A N D H O N E Y
E O E L O X D C A A S I S T A
S R T G H C C O R B A U Z I Y
L L B W A K A B R A H A M A N
```

THE CROSSING OF THE RED SEA
EXODUS 14:21-23, 26-31

And Moses stretched out his hand over the sea; and the LORD caused the sea to go back by a strong _ _ _ _ _ _ _ _ (2w) all that night, and made the sea _ _ _ _ _ _ _ (2w), and the waters were _ _ _ _ _ _ _. **22** And the children of Israel went into the midst of the sea upon the dry _ _ _ _ _ _: and the waters were a wall unto them on their right hand, and on their _ _ _ _. **23** And the Egyptians pursued, and went in after them to the midst of the sea, even all Pharaoh's horses, his _ _ _ _ _ _ _ _, and his _ _ _ _ _ _ _ _ _. . . . **26** And the LORD said unto _ _ _ _ _, Stretch out thine hand over the sea, that the waters may come again upon the _ _ _ _ _ _ _ _ _, upon their chariots, and upon their horsemen. **27** And Moses stretched forth his hand over the sea, and the sea returned to his strength when the _ _ _ _ _ _ _ appeared; and the Egyptians fled against it; and the LORD _ _ _ _ _ _ _ _ _ _ the Egyptians in the midst of the sea. **28** And the waters returned, and _ _ _ _ _ _ _ _ the chariots, and the horsemen, and all the host of _ _ _ _ _ _ _ that came into the sea after them; there remained not so much as one of them. **29** But the children of _ _ _ _ _ _ walked upon dry land in the midst of the sea; and the waters were a wall unto them on their _ _ _ _ _ hand, and on their left. **30** Thus the LORD _ _ _ _ _ _ Israel that day out of the _ _ _ _ of the Egyptians; and Israel saw the Egyptians dead upon the _ _ _ _ _ _ _ _ _ (2w). **31** And Israel saw that great work which the LORD did upon the Egyptians: and the people _ _ _ _ _ _ _ the LORD, and _ _ _ _ _ _ _ _ _ the LORD, and his servant Moses.

```
G Y B S I R L O G F A I N G D
G D E R E V O C D N A L Y R D
D O L A O R M I S R A E L O N
N O I P S A V E D O B E H U I
C M E Z Y I S L N Y F O E N W
H R V S D P S P A T A V B D T
A X E E N Q U A H R W E P I S
R S D A G E S G A T U R G D A
I E S S B Y I H R T H T C K E
O S T H X R P P H K C H Y M C
T O V O R Q U T F E A R E D K
S M O R N I N G I R E E N F A
R M N E A Q U H D A F W R B L
A G H R A I N A Z T N C H U T
B T G L L Z G N E M E S R O H
```

SAMUEL'S CALLING
1 SAMUEL 3:2-11, 19-21

And it came to pass at that time, when Eli was laid down in his place, and his eyes began to _ _ _ _ _ _ (2w), that he could not see; **3** And ere the _ _ _ _ of God went out in the _ _ _ _ _ _ of the LORD, where the ark of God was, and Samuel was laid down to sleep; **4** That the LORD called _ _ _ _ _ _: and he answered, Here am I. **5** And he ran unto Eli, and said, _ _ _ _ _ _ _ (3w); for thou calledst me. And he said, I called not; lie down again. And he went and _ _ _ _ _ _ _ (2w). **6** And the LORD called yet again, Samuel. And Samuel _ _ _ _ _ _ and went to Eli, and said, Here am I; for thou didst call me. And he answered, I called not, my son; lie down again. **7** Now Samuel did not yet know the LORD, neither was the word of the LORD yet _ _ _ _ _ _ _ _ _ unto him. **8** And the LORD called Samuel again the _ _ _ _ _ _ time. And he arose and went to Eli, and said, Here am I; for thou didst call me. And Eli _ _ _ _ _ _ _ _ _ _ that the LORD had called the child. **9** Therefore Eli said unto Samuel, Go, lie down: and it shall be, if he call thee, that thou shalt say, _ _ _ _ _, LORD; for thy _ _ _ _ _ _ _ heareth. So Samuel went and lay down in his place. **10** And the LORD came, and stood, and called as at other times, Samuel, Samuel. Then Samuel answered, Speak; for thy servant _ _ _ _ _ _ _ _. **11** And the LORD said to Samuel, Behold, I will do a thing in _ _ _ _ _ _ _, at which both the ears of every one that heareth it shall _ _ _ _ _ _ _. . . . **19** And Samuel _ _ _ _ _, and the LORD was with him, and did let none of his words fall to the ground. **20** And all Israel from Dan even to _ _ _ _ _ _ _ _ _ knew

```
E D E I L N V E R E W D Z N G
C H R C U S S H I L O H H R S
D I K D E L A E V E R U S B O
E T M D A S T L M I D X A W N
V R L A Y D O W N T O N R A O
I S R A E L G O H O F S O N D
E S S P L R Y F U B T T S L L
C E B N E O E T Q Y H P E E X
R R S W A B E H S R E E B E T
E V A E N M U I L A L L R I U
P A M S P D D R K A O G L D A
P N U L T T O D M O R N D F L
Z T E H P O R P P I D I N E S
F I L A P T H E A R E T H O G
N G A M D A U L T H G T D N E
```

that Samuel was established to be a _ _ _ _ _ _ _ _ of the LORD. **21** And the LORD appeared again in _ _ _ _ _ _: for the LORD revealed himself to Samuel in Shiloh by the _ _ _ _ _ _ _ _ _ _ _ _ _ (4w).

17

DAVID AND GOLIATH
1 SAMUEL 17:45-51

Then said David to the _ _ _ _ _ _ _ _ _ _, Thou comest to me with a _ _ _ _ _, and with a spear, and with a shield: but I come to thee in the name of the LORD of hosts, the God of the armies of _ _ _ _ _ _, whom thou hast _ _ _ _ _ _. **46** This day will the LORD _ _ _ _ _ _ _ _ thee into mine hand; and I will _ _ _ _ _ _ _ _ _ _ (2w), and take thine head from thee; and I will give the carcases of the host of the Philistines this day unto the fowls of the air, and to the wild _ _ _ _ _ _ of the earth; that all the earth may know that there is a God in Israel. **47** And all this _ _ _ _ _ _ _ _ _ shall know that the LORD saveth not with sword and _ _ _ _ _: for the battle is the LORD's, and he will give you _ _ _ _ _ _ _ _ _ _ _ _ (3w). **48** And it came to pass, when the Philistine arose, and came, and drew nigh to meet David, that David hastened, and ran toward the _ _ _ _ to meet the Philistine. **49** And David put his hand in his bag, and took thence a _ _ _ _ _ _, and slang it, and smote the Philistine in his forehead, that the stone sunk into his _ _ _ _ _ _ _ _; and he fell upon his face to the earth. **50** So David _ _ _ _ _ _ _ _ _ _ over the Philistine with a _ _ _ _ _ _ and with a stone, and smote the Philistine, and slew him; but there was no sword in the hand of David. **51** Therefore David ran, and _ _ _ _ _ _ _ _ _ _ (2w) the Philistine, and took his sword, and drew it out of the _ _ _ _ _ _ _ thereof, and slew him, and _ _ _ _ _ _ _ _ _ _ _ _ _ (4w) therewith. And when the Philistines saw their _ _ _ _ _ _ _ _ _ was _ _ _ _ _, they fled.

```
R E V I L E D E L I A V E R P
L E D A E H S I H F F O T U C
S H E A T H C F A V C E I T R
S A A O E S T O N E E N D A I
P W D K I D W A S H T Y E R A
Y C O H V N L O B A R P F M R
A H S T S A E B R I S H I Y R
E A A N T H C K T D H I E H E
D M L F O R E H E A D L D I S
R P O R H U G E L F Y I N N N
T I O X E O Y L B M E S S A K
N O P U D O O T S R D T L E O
F N S Z D T L E A R S I I F U
R H U C E N A Y C B T N N W D
M O Q S M I T E T H E E G N R
```

18

DANIEL AND THE LIONS' DEN
DANIEL 6:16–23, 28

Then the king _ _ _ _ _ _ _ _ _, and they brought Daniel, and cast him into the _ _ _ _ _ _ _ _ _ _ (3w). Now the king spake and said unto Daniel, Thy God whom thou servest continually, he will _ _ _ _ _ _ _ _ _ _ _ (2w). **17** And a _ _ _ _ _ was brought, and laid upon the mouth of the den; and the king sealed it with his own _ _ _ _ _ _, and with the signet of his lords; that the purpose might not be changed concerning Daniel. **18** Then the king went to his _ _ _ _ _ _, and passed the night _ _ _ _ _ _ _: neither were _ _ _ _ _ _ _ _ _ _ _ _ of musick brought before him: and his sleep went from him. **19** Then the king arose very early in the _ _ _ _ _ _ _, and went in haste unto the den of lions. **20** And when he came to the den, he cried with a _ _ _ _ _ _ _ _ _ _ _ voice unto Daniel: and the king spake and said to _ _ _ _ _ _ _, O Daniel, servant of the living God, is thy God, whom thou servest _ _ _ _ _ _ _ _ _ _ _ _, able to deliver thee from the lions? **21** Then said Daniel unto the king, O king, _ _ _ _ _ _ _ _ _ _ _ (3w). **22** My God hath sent his _ _ _ _ _, and hath shut the lions' _ _ _ _ _ _, that they have not hurt me: forasmuch as before him innocency was found in me; and also before thee, O king, have I done no hurt. **23** Then was the king _ _ _ _ _ _ _ _ _ _ _ _ _ _ _ (2w) for him, and commanded that they should take Daniel up out of the den. So Daniel was taken up out of the den, and no manner of hurt was found upon him, because he believed in his God. . . . **28** So this

```
I A P S F E N R G N I T S A F
E R A I N S T R U M E N T S R
D A L G Y L G N I D E E C X E
E T A N G E L O E E K B O K V
N B C E J O G D E L U Q N I E
O C E T E P N A L I G L T V R
F R A C R A I R B V U N I H O
L A U I M H N I A E P W N A F
I T H M T R R U T R E Z U D E
O E O S S T O S N T R Z A J V
N C D T T H M A E H S N L L I
S H T U O M W R M E I E L P L
S Y S I N I T X A E A A Y U C
G O S R E P R O L F N B D E T
M D O C R D E R E P S O R P N
```

Daniel _ _ _ _ _ _ _ _ _ _ in the reign of _ _ _ _ _ _, and in the reign
of Cyrus the _ _ _ _ _ _ _ _.

19

THE TOWER OF BABEL
GENESIS 11:1-9

And the whole earth was of one _ _ _ _ _ _ _ _, and of one speech. **2** And it _ _ _ _ _ _ _ _ _ _ (3w), as they journeyed from the east, that they found a plain in the land of _ _ _ _ _ _; and they dwelt there. **3** And they said one to _ _ _ _ _ _ _, Go to, let us make _ _ _ _ _, and burn them thoroughly. And they had brick for stone, and slime had they for morter. **4** And they said, Go to, let us _ _ _ _ _ us a city and a _ _ _ _ _, whose top may reach unto _ _ _ _ _ _; and let us make us a name, lest we be scattered abroad upon the face of the whole _ _ _ _ _. **5** And the LORD came down to see the _ _ _ _ and the tower, which the _ _ _ _ _ _ _ _ _ _ _ _ _ (3w) builded. **6** And the LORD said, Behold, the _ _ _ _ _ _ is one, and they have all one language; and this they begin to do: and now nothing will be restrained from them, which they have _ _ _ _ _ _ _ _ to do. **7** Go to, let us go down, and there _ _ _ _ _ _ _ _ their language, that they may not _ _ _ _ _ _ _ _ _ _ _ one another's _ _ _ _ _ _. **8** So the LORD _ _ _ _ _ _ _ _ _ them abroad from thence upon the _ _ _ _ of all the earth: and they left off to build the city. **9** Therefore is the name of it called _ _ _ _ _; because the LORD did there confound the language of all the earth: and from thence did the LORD scatter them _ _ _ _ _ _ upon the face of all the earth.

```
C I F S S A P O T E M A C Y H
S Y E H B J I C K T W E H T U
K U N I A U E C T X I L I T N
E F E N L P I R P E O P L E D
W A G A S R B L E D L E D N E
K C I R B K F A D A E R R E R
L E I O P A D Y N N B S E H S
P H V T T E N G E O A R N T T
A L N N Y N U W H T B E O R A
C K A R P A O R S H S W F A N
H I S H G L F I R E E A M E D
D D N E M U N L E R S N E I T
I S E I K Q O H E A V E N T I
H C E E P S C A T T E R E D S
N T D E N I G A M I M E I M F
```

JACOB'S LADDER
GENESIS 28:10-13, 15-16, 18-22

And Jacob went out from _ _ _ _ _ _ _ _ _, and went toward Haran. **11** And he lighted upon a certain place, and tarried there all night, because the sun was set; and he took of the stones of that place, and put them for his pillows, and lay down in that place to sleep. **12** And he _ _ _ _ _ _ _, and behold a _ _ _ _ _ _ set up on the earth, and the top of it reached to _ _ _ _ _ _: and behold the _ _ _ _ _ _ of God ascending and _ _ _ _ _ _ _ _ _ _ on it. **13** And, behold, the LORD stood above it, and said, I am the LORD God of _ _ _ _ _ _ _ thy father, and the God of _ _ _ _ _: the land whereon thou liest, to thee will I give it, and to thy seed. . . . **15** And, behold, _ _ _ _ _ _ _ _ _ _ _ (4w), and will keep thee in all places whither thou goest, and will bring thee again into this land; for I will not leave thee, until I have done that which I have spoken to thee of. **16** And _ _ _ _ _ awaked out of his _ _ _ _ _, and he said, Surely the LORD is _ _ _ _ _ _ _ _ _ _ (3w); and I knew it not. . . . **18** And Jacob rose up early in the morning, and took the stone that he had put for his _ _ _ _ _ _ _ _, and set it up for a pillar, and poured oil upon the top of it. **19** And he called the name of that place _ _ _ _ _ _: but the name of that city was called Luz at the first. **20** And Jacob _ _ _ _ _ a vow, saying, If God will be with me, and will keep me in this way that I go, and will give me _ _ _ _ _ _ _ _ _ _ _ (3w), and raiment to put on, **21** So that I come again to my father's house in _ _ _ _ _; then shall the LORD _ _ _ _ _ _ _ (3w): **22** And this stone, which I have set for a

```
G N I D N E C S E D E W O V N
A K N P E R T E N T H E U Q R
C T T A E O T D A E R B B B T T
W A H C B A E I H E A V E N N
P E I R G R W T D S F R E Y Z
H R S P S B A D E M A E R D E
C A P T O R A H C N H A S O Y
N Y L C D L A I A T E Q H G S
E E A S T G E L H M C U E Y E
R J C L H A P T L R A I B M N
S L E E P H I N F I E E A E A
D B Z G S W O L L I P A C B S
E E C N M R I C A A S I O P U
G E K A X T E E A S S R Y W M
L L I E G E R N B E T H E L B
```

_ _ _ _ _ _, shall be God's house: and of all that thou shalt give me I will surely give the _ _ _ _ _ unto thee.

21

DAVID CHOSEN BY GOD
1 SAMUEL 16:1, 6–13

And the LORD said unto Samuel, How long wilt thou mourn for Saul, seeing I have rejected him from _ _ _ _ _ _ _ _ over Israel? fill thine _ _ _ _ _ _ _ _ _ _ _ (3w), and go, I will send thee to Jesse the _ _ _ _ _ _ _ _ _ _ _ _: for I have provided me a king among his sons. . . . **6** And it came to pass, when they were come, that he looked on Eliab, and said, Surely the LORD's _ _ _ _ _ _ _ _ is before him. **7** But the LORD said unto _ _ _ _ _ _, Look not on his countenance, or on the _ _ _ _ _ _ of his stature; because I have _ _ _ _ _ _ _ _ him: for the LORD seeth not as man seeth; for man looketh on the _ _ _ _ _ _ _ appearance, but the LORD looketh on the _ _ _ _ _. **8** Then Jesse called Abinadab, and made him pass before Samuel. And he said, Neither hath the _ _ _ _ chosen this. **9** Then _ _ _ _ _ _ made Shammah to pass by. And he said, Neither hath the LORD _ _ _ _ _ _ _ _ _ _ _ (2w). **10** Again, Jesse made seven _ _ _ _ _ _ _ _ _ (3w) to pass before Samuel. And Samuel said unto Jesse, The Lord hath not chosen these. **11** And Samuel said unto Jesse, Are here all thy _ _ _ _ _ _ _ _ _? And he said, There remaineth yet the _ _ _ _ _ _ _ _, and, behold, he keepeth the sheep. And Samuel said unto Jesse, Send and _ _ _ _ _ _ _ _ (2w): for we will not sit down till he come hither. **12** And he sent, and brought him in. Now he was ruddy, and withal of a beautiful _ _ _ _ _ _ _ _ _ _ _ _, and goodly to look to. And the LORD said, Arise, _ _ _ _ _ _ him: for this is he. **13** Then Samuel took the horn of oil,

```
D A V I D R A W T U O S T R O
R E I G N I N G A D I R C K M
O T H T Z Q X B T I O H S E I
L H E I U U Q E A R N Y G P H
E V A O S I H T N E S O H C H
H O R N W I T H O I L U E O C
T F T D Y W E L I N R N I U T
F C H I L D R E N T E G G N E
O E L Y U E O H T L F E H T F
T D K T Q S U E E J U S T E S
I W H P E W D M D E S T O N V
R H C I N R P I A S E P W A E
I I A N O I N T Y S D H E N M
P R E L S F O E E E H G I C F
S N O S S I H F O H C T C E O
```

and anointed him in the midst of his brethren: and the _ _ _ _ _ _ _ _ _
_ _ _ _ _ _ _ (4w) came upon _ _ _ _ _ from that day forward.

THE BATTLE OF JERICHO
JOSHUA 6:12-16, 20-21

And Joshua rose early in the _ _ _ _ _ _ _, and the priests took up the ark of the LORD. **13** And seven _ _ _ _ _ _ _ bearing _ _ _ _ _ _ _ _ _ _ _ (2w) of rams' horns before the _ _ _ _ _ _ _ _ _ _ _ _ _ (4w) went on continually, and _ _ _ _ with the trumpets: and the armed men went before them; but the rereward came after the ark of the LORD, the priests going on, and _ _ _ _ _ _ _ with the trumpets. **14** And the second day they compassed the city once, and returned into the camp: so they did _ _ _ _ _ _ _ (2w). **15** And it came to pass on the _ _ _ _ _ _ _ day, that they _ _ _ _ early about the _ _ _ _ _ _ _ _ _ _ _ _ _ _ (4w), and _ _ _ _ _ _ _ _ _ _ the city after the same manner seven times: only on that day they compassed the city seven times. **16** And it came to pass at the seventh time, when the priests blew with the trumpets, _ _ _ _ _ _ said unto the people, _ _ _ _ _; for the LORD hath given you the city. . . . **20** So the people _ _ _ _ _ _ _ _ when the priests blew with the trumpets: and it _ _ _ _ _ _ _ _ _ _ _ (3w), when the people heard the sound of the trumpet, and the people shouted with a _ _ _ _ _ _ _ _ _ _ (2w), that the wall _ _ _ _ _ _ _ _ _ _ _ _ (3w), so that the _ _ _ _ _ _ went up into the city, every man straight before him, and they took the city. **21** And they _ _ _ _ _ _ _ _ _ _ _ _ _ _ _ _ all that was in the city.

```
A K N N S D E Y O R T S E D A
T U O H S T A E R G A H S A S
P R I E S T S O P U P O W W T
M Y O F A C S H H I L U H N E
K M H W E E R S S G N T C I P
S E C C Z L O I E B L E W N M
S H O U T J L X A V I D G G U
A M M O Q U G D T Q E N K O R
P L P Y G U H A O U I N C F T
O L A R N T P Y I W H R T T N
T M S D I T R S O U N S E H E
E L S G N E A L Y L E F L E V
M K E H R R B N D L M O L D E
A F D R O L E H T F O K R A S
C F R E M Y P E O P L E C Y T
```

23

SHADRACH, MESHACH, AND ABEDNEGO

DANIEL 3:14-25

Nebuchadnezzar spake and said unto them, Is it true, O Shadrach, Meshach, and Abednego, do not ye serve my gods, nor worship the _ _ _ _ _ _ _ _ _ _ _ (2w) which I have set up? **15** Now if ye be ready that at what time ye hear the sound of the cornet, _ _ _ _ _, harp, sackbut, psaltery, and _ _ _ _ _ _ _ _, and all kinds of musick, ye fall down and _ _ _ _ _ _ _ the image which I have made; well: but if ye worship not, ye shall be cast the same hour into the midst of a burning _ _ _ _ _ _ _ _ _ _ _ (2w); and who is that God that shall _ _ _ _ _ _ _ you out of my hands? **16** _ _ _ _ _ _ _ _ _, _ _ _ _ _ _ _ _, and _ _ _ _ _ _ _ _, answered and said to the king, O _ _ _ _ _ _ _ _ _ _ _ _ _ _ _, we are not careful to answer thee in this matter. **17** If it be so, our God whom we _ _ _ _ _ is able to deliver us from the burning fiery furnace, and he will deliver us out of thine hand, O king. **18** But if not, be it known unto thee, _ _ _ _ _ (2w), that we will not serve thy gods, nor worship the golden image which thou hast set up. **19** Then was Nebuchadnezzar full of _ _ _ _, and the form of his visage was changed against Shadrach, Meshach, and Abednego: therefore he spake, and commanded that they should heat the furnace one _ _ _ _ _ times more than it was wont to be heated. **20** And he _ _ _ _ _ _ _ _ _ _ the most _ _ _ _ _ _ men that were in his army to bind Shadrach, Meshach, and Abednego, and to cast them into the burning fiery furnace. **21** Then these men were bound in their coats, their hosen, and their hats, and their other _ _ _ _ _ _ _ _,

```
B E C A N R U F Y R E I F S H
G O L D E N I M A G E E N A I
Y S P A N E M E E R H T W B E
I R A Z Z E N D A H C U B E N
W O R S H I P S E D T L I D L
T L V U Q F E H E B H F S N N
S L M E U R T D B V W E I E O
H E M G V H N U O M E P K G S
A S A E R A H L O K I N G O T
D N L L M I C C P H S X N J N
R U H M I N A I B D E O L E E
A O O C G O H M C A F S T M M
C C A Z H L S E K G N N C H R
H I F F T P E R O M S I L E A
O F U R Y V M D E L I V E R G
```

and were cast into the midst of the burning fiery furnace. . . . **24** Then Nebuchadnezzar the king was astonished, and rose up in haste, and spake, and said unto his _ _ _ _ _ _ _ _ _ _ _, Did not we cast _ _ _ _ _ _ _ _ (2w) bound into the midst of the fire? They answered and said unto the king, _ _ _ _, O king. **25** He answered and said, Lo, I see four men loose, walking in the midst of the fire, and they have no hurt; and the form of the fourth is like the _ _ _ _ _ _ _ _ (3w).

24

JOSEPH'S COAT OF MANY COLORS
GENESIS 37:3-5, 17-18, 23-24, 28-34

Now _ _ _ _ _ _ loved Joseph more than all his _ _ _ _ _ _ _ _, because he was the son of his old age: and he made him a coat of many colours. **4** And when his brethren saw that their _ _ _ _ _ _ loved him more than all his brethren, they _ _ _ _ _ _ _ _ _ (2w), and could not speak _ _ _ _ _ _ _ _ _ _ unto him. **5** And Joseph _ _ _ _ _ _ _ a dream, and he told it his brethren: and they hated him yet the more. . . . **17** And Joseph went after his _ _ _ _ _ _ _ _, and found them in _ _ _ _ _ _. **18** And when they saw him afar off, even before he came near unto them, they _ _ _ _ _ _ _ _ _ _ against him to slay him. . . . **23** And it came to pass, when _ _ _ _ _ _ _ was come unto his brethren, that they stript Joseph out of his _ _ _ _, his coat of many colours that was on him; **24** And they took him, and cast him _ _ _ _ _ _ _ _ (3w): and the pit was empty, there was no _ _ _ _ _ in it. . . . **28** Then there passed by Midianites _ _ _ _ _ _ _ _ _ _ _ _; and they drew and lifted up Joseph out of the pit, and sold Joseph to the Ishmeelites for twenty pieces of _ _ _ _ _ _: and they brought Joseph into _ _ _ _ _. . . . **31** And they took Joseph's coat, and killed a kid of the _ _ _ _ _, and dipped the coat in the blood; **32** And they sent the coat of many colours, and they brought it to their father; and said, This have we found: know now whether it be thy son's coat or no. **33** And he knew it, and said, It is my son's coat; an _ _ _ _ _ _ _ _ _ (2w) hath devoured him; Joseph is without doubt rent in pieces. **34** And Jacob rent his clothes, and put _ _ _ _ _ _ _ _ upon his loins, and _ _ _ _ _ _ _ for his son many days.

```
N E R D L I H C N A I V Y O H
A H A T E D H I M Z C L R E T
H I B I X L E S E S I L V E R
T W D R T H F R R S T A O G Z
O P R E R P E A C E A B L Y L
D N E E N I N E H C K Q U P I
E Q A S T R G L A P R H I T H
R U M Z H X U B N C E U N I R
I A E R S L A O T L T S T K Y
P T D C A L L H M R A C O C S
S C O I O E S P E R W H A J T
N M A B L A V H N S N I P S T
O I A B R E T H R E N J I X B
C N B T S A E B L I V E T E U
C G R E F S A C K C L O T H L
```

25

THE GOLDEN CALF
EXODUS 32:7-8, 15-20

And the LORD said unto Moses, Go, get thee down; for thy _ _ _ _ _ _, which thou broughtest out of the land of _ _ _ _ _, have corrupted themselves: **8** They have turned aside quickly out of the way which I _ _ _ _ _ _ _ _ _ them: they have made them a molten _ _ _ _, and have worshipped it, and have sacrificed thereunto, and said, These be thy gods, _ _ _ _ _ _ _ (2w), which have brought thee up out of the land of Egypt. . . . **15** And _ _ _ _ _ turned, and went down from the _ _ _ _ _, and the two tables of the _ _ _ _ _ _ _ _ _ were in his hand: the _ _ _ _ _ _ were written on both their sides; on the one side and on the other were they _ _ _ _ _ _ _. **16** And the tables were the work of God, and the writing was the writing of God, _ _ _ _ _ _ upon the tables. **17** And when Joshua heard the noise of the people as they shouted, he said unto Moses, There is a _ _ _ _ _ _ _ _ _ _ (3w) in the camp. **18** And he said, It is not the voice of them that shout for mastery, neither is it the voice of them that cry for being _ _ _ _ _ _ _ _: but the noise of them that sing do I hear. **19** And it came to pass, as soon as he came nigh unto the _ _ _ _, that he saw the calf, and the _ _ _ _ _ _ _: and Moses' anger _ _ _ _ _ hot, and he cast the tables out of his _ _ _ _ _, and brake them beneath the mount. **20** And he took the calf which they had made, and burnt it in the _ _ _ _, and ground it to _ _ _ _ _ _, and strawed it upon the water, and made the children of Israel _ _ _ _ _ _ _ _ _ (3w).

```
E G N I C N A D S P E E H I C
M A E D A G W A X E D T R L A
O S I P L R M O D R T N U O M
C D E D N A M M O C O T B E P
R T P O E V E A E I W O D N E
E G Y P T E N V S P S L S I E
V D C Q T N E E H C B R N T S
O R P U I A O R Y A E G A R Y
B I S O R F N I A L O B A E E
R N K A W O M B P F L Y R W L
A K T A L D S O K E B I R V A
L O R E Y I E S S R F T I O N
H F O G I P T R U E D O J H E
T I H Z Y N O M I T S E T C R
G T E H A N D S N E U A M K T
```

THE PROMISE OF ISAAC
GENESIS 17: 1–9, 15–19

And when Abram was ninety years old and nine, the LORD appeared to _ _ _ _ _, and said unto him, I am the _ _ _ _ _ _ _ _ _ _ _ (2w); walk before me, and be thou _ _ _ _ _ _ _. **2** And I will make my _ _ _ _ _ _ _ _ between me and thee, and will _ _ _ _ _ _ _ _ thee exceedingly. **3** And Abram fell on his face: and God talked with him, saying, **4** As for me, behold, my covenant is with thee, and thou shalt be a father of many _ _ _ _ _ _ _. **5** Neither shall thy name any more be called Abram, but thy name shall be _ _ _ _ _ _ _; for a father of many nations have I made thee. **6** And I will make thee exceeding fruitful, and I will make nations of thee, and _ _ _ _ _ shall come out of thee. **7** And I will establish my covenant _ _ _ _ _ _ _ me and thee and thy seed after thee in their generations for an _ _ _ _ _ _ _ _ _ _ _ covenant, to be a God unto thee, and to thy seed after thee. **8** And I will give unto thee, and to thy seed after thee, the land wherein thou art a _ _ _ _ _ _ _ _, all the land of Canaan, for an everlasting _ _ _ _ _ _ _ _ _ _ _; and I will be their God. **9** And God said unto Abraham, Thou shalt keep my covenant therefore, thou, and thy seed after thee in their _ _ _ _ _ _ _ _ _ _ _ _. . . . **15** And God said unto Abraham, As for Sarai thy _ _ _ _ _, thou shalt not call her name Sarai, but _ _ _ _ _ shall her name be. **16** And I will bless her, and give thee a son also of her: yea, I will bless her, and she shall be a _ _ _ _ _ _ _ of nations; kings of people shall be of her. **17** Then Abraham fell upon his face, and _ _ _ _ _ _ _, and said in his heart, Shall a child

```
L A U G H E D L M S E R Y G O
N L O P I E G I T C E F R E P
A M O T H E R E V O R E D N O
T I I G N I T S A L R E V E S
I G N S P I S H N G R N I R S
O H E F I W A E I D S E R A E
N T W A R Q U W N T M E A T S
S Y L P I T L U M W O W T I S
D G O I S C H C E A N T H O I
C O V E N A N T E K R E R N O
O D H I L B E C X E X B K S N
N M A H A R B A D G I F A I L
U B C H I R B A C H S R B P E
R E G N A R T S K W A T E I P
E Y L F S G N I K H T P H B A
```

be born unto him that is an _ _ _ _ _ _ _ _ years old? and shall Sarah, that is ninety years old, bear? **18** And Abraham said unto God, O that Ishmael might live before thee! **19** And God said, Sarah thy wife shall bear thee a son indeed; and thou shalt call his name _ _ _ _ _: and I will establish my covenant with him for an everlasting covenant, and with his seed after him.

JACOB WRESTLES WITH THE ANGEL
GENESIS 32:22-31

And [Jacob] rose up that _ _ _ _ _, and took his two wives, and his two _ _ _ _ _ _ _ _ _ _ _ _ _, and his eleven sons, and passed over the ford Jabbok. **23** And he took them, and sent them over the brook, and sent over that he had. **24** And _ _ _ _ _ was left alone; and there _ _ _ _ _ _ _ _ a man with him until the _ _ _ _ _ _ _ _ of the day. **25** And when he saw that he _ _ _ _ _ _ _ _ _ not against him, he touched the hollow of his _ _ _ _ _; and the hollow of Jacob's thigh was _ _ _ _ _ _ _ _ _ _ (3w), as he wrestled with him. **26** And he said, _ _ _ _ _ _ _ _ (3w), for the day breaketh. And he said, I will not let thee go, except thou _ _ _ _ _ _ _ (2w). **27** And he said unto him, What is thy _ _ _ _? And he said, Jacob. **28** And he said, Thy name shall be called no more Jacob, but _ _ _ _ _ _ _: for as a prince hast thou _ _ _ _ _ with God and with _ _ _, and hast prevailed. **29** And Jacob _ _ _ _ _ him, and said, Tell me, _ _ _ _ _ _ _ _ _ (3w), thy name. And he said, Wherefore is it that thou dost ask after my name? And he blessed him there. **30** And Jacob called the name of the place _ _ _ _ _ _ _: for I have seen God _ _ _ _ _ _ _ _ _ _ (3w), and my life is _ _ _ _ _ _ _ _ _ _. **31** And as he passed over Penuel the _ _ _ rose upon him, and he halted upon his thigh.

```
T G E K E O V H A N O N E R W
V A O R R R U Q E U A A T H S H
L S S F L L D S E M S S E L B
E U B A B E T J L E T N O P I
G P R O K Y N H E N N F S M P
F W E S C R I G T G A I I S R
L D A T U A O I M C V S G S A
O E K D S O J H E U R R E H Y
L V I U E K F T G S E A P L T
E R N Y A L O T O E S E U O H
I E G W I F T J D L N L R W E
N S G O A U U S A V E I C P E
E E H C S Q O N E U M A K H N
P R E V A I L E D R O E I R B
L P O F O T E R P O W E R T O
```

28

ELIJAH AND BAAL
1 KINGS 18:31-39

And Elijah took twelve _ _ _ _ _ _, according to the number of the tribes of the _ _ _ _ _ _ _ _ _ _ _ (3w), unto whom the word of the LORD came, saying, Israel shall be thy name: **32** And with the stones he built an _ _ _ _ _ in the name of the LORD: and he made a _ _ _ _ _ _ about the altar, as great as would contain two measures of seed. **33** And he put the _ _ _ _ in order, and cut the _ _ _ _ _ _ _ in pieces, and laid him on the wood, and said, Fill four _ _ _ _ _ _ _ with water, and pour it on the burnt _ _ _ _ _ _ _ _ _, and on the wood. **34** And he said, Do it the second time. And they did it the second time. And he said, Do it the third time. And they did it the _ _ _ _ _ time. **35** And the water ran round about the altar; and he filled the trench also with _ _ _ _ _. **36** And it _ _ _ _ _ _ _ _ _ _ (3w) at the time of the offering of the evening sacrifice, that Elijah the _ _ _ _ _ _ _ came near, and said, LORD God of Abraham, _ _ _ _ _, and of Israel, let it be known this day that thou art God in _ _ _ _ _ _, and that I am thy _ _ _ _ _ _ _, and that I have done all these things at thy word. **37** _ _ _ _ _ _ (2w), O LORD, hear me, that this people may know that thou art the _ _ _ _ _ _ _ (2w), and that thou hast turned their heart back again. **38** Then the _ _ _ _ of the LORD fell, and consumed the burnt sacrifice, and the wood, and the stones, and the dust, and _ _ _ _ _ _ up the water that was in the trench. **39** And when all the people saw it, they fell on their _ _ _ _ _: and they said, The LORD, he is the God; the LORD, he is the God.

```
U T W L A T I N E W N O I C I
S T O N E S L G O E R C T S H
Q E H P R O E P T N A V R E S
U H C E G N A T D A N E I C A
S P A Y E S R H S E V G N A K
O O M D E O S I L O K K H F A
A R E C I F I R C A S C F M R
U P T M T J T D I T N O I Y E
G R O E O A I P U E A L R L R
A Z P N W C L Q R H N L E O U
N D A M A O H T P E M U C R L
U F S G T B O S A A E B I D A
L A S S E Y V D O R D I T G C
S L E R R A B C K M E P R O L
Y T H F T H K H C E A A G D I
```

RAHAB AND THE SPIES
JOSHUA 2:1, 3-4, 6, 15-17, 18-21

And Joshua the _ _ _ _ _ _ _ _ (3w) sent out of Shittim two men to _ _ _ secretly, saying, Go view the land, even _ _ _ _ _ _ _. And they went, and came into an harlot's house, named Rahab, and lodged there. . . . **3** And the king of Jericho sent unto _ _ _ _ _, saying, Bring forth the men that are come to thee, which are entered into thine _ _ _ _ _: for they be come to search out all the _ _ _ _ _ _ _. **4** And the woman took the _ _ _ _ _ _ (2w), and hid them. . . . **6** But she had brought them up to the _ _ _ _ of the house, and hid them with the stalks of _ _ _ _, which she had laid in order upon the roof. . . . **15** Then she let them down by a cord through the _ _ _ _ _ _: for her house was upon the town _ _ _ _, and she dwelt upon the wall. **16** And she said unto them, Get you to the _ _ _ _ _ _ _ _, lest the pursuers meet you; and hide yourselves there _ _ _ _ _ _ _ _ _ (2w), until the pursuers be returned: and afterward may ye go your way. **17** And the men said unto her. . . . **18** Behold, when we come into the land, thou shalt bind this line of _ _ _ _ _ _ _ thread in the window which thou didst let us down by: and thou shalt bring thy father, and thy mother, and thy brethren, and all thy father's _ _ _ _ _ _ _ _ _ _, home unto thee. **19** And it shall be, that whosoever shall go out of the _ _ _ _ _ of thy house into the street, his _ _ _ _ _ shall be upon his head, and we will be guiltless: and whosoever shall be with thee in the house, his blood shall be on our head, if any hand be upon him. **20** And if thou utter this our _ _ _ _ _ _ _ _ _, then we will be quit of thine oath which thou

```
I N C E X P P I B K E R I O E
R I S E E O S W D G T O N N V
E A A L W O R D S R A H A B Q
O T T A I A U M E N O C Y L U
M N U G N F L A X U O I I O M
S U C H D A Y L S N B R K O M
H O T T O K I E T F L E T D B
I M O N W C H X P O O J H P U
E N W I O O O N S N Q U R T S
R C G N L U M J H O U S E R I
S T R D D N L E D S P Z E S N
Y H H E O T A V N Y C K D R E
Z E F O O R E A T E L R A C S
B I Y R R Y I G C K S H Y P S
W N T E S O C R H A T M S A G
```

hast made us to swear. **21** And she said, According unto your _ _ _ _ _ _ ,
so be it. And she sent them away, and they departed: and she bound
the scarlet line in the window.

30

THE CROSSING OF THE JORDAN

JOSHUA 3:5, 14–17

And Joshua said unto the people, _ _ _ _ _ _ _ _ yourselves: for to morrow the LORD will do _ _ _ _ _ _ _ among you. . . . **14** And it _ _ _ _ _ _ _ _ _ _ (3w), when the _ _ _ _ _ _ removed from their _ _ _ _ _, to pass over Jordan, and the priests bearing the ark _ _ _ _ _ _ _ _ _ _ _ _ _(3w) before the people; **15** And as they that bare the ark were come unto _ _ _ _ _ _, and the feet of the _ _ _ _ _ _ _ that bare the ark were dipped in the brim of the _ _ _ _ _, (for Jordan overfloweth all his banks all the time of _ _ _ _ _ _ _,) **16** That the waters which came down from _ _ _ _ _ stood and rose up upon an heap very far from the city _ _ _ _, that is beside Zaretan: and those that came down toward the sea of the plain, even the _ _ _ _ _ _ _ (2w), failed, and were cut off: and the people _ _ _ _ _ _ over right against _ _ _ _ _ _ _. **17** And the priests that bare the _ _ _ of the covenant of the _ _ _ _ stood firm on _ _ _ _ _ _ _ _ (2w) in the midst of Jordan, and all the _ _ _ _ _ _ _ _ _ _ passed over on dry ground, until all the people were passed _ _ _ _ _ over Jordan.

```
L F W T H E R O L W L H L T C
L O C S E T I L E A R S I E I
B S S R N M E A I T B H I V L
O Y S A M O G H J E O R O O L
H M A R N T N O T R V E A B F
F E P K E C R L C D E S S A P
D R O L S D T E C L H F L V E
R X T O A I N I P P E P N I D
Y G E N D R O O F P N A N H S
G Q M P A T E P W Y I O N A N
R U A O M P R I E S T S B R R
O H C I R E J C H S T T S V T
U R E Y C M B A E L S N H E S
N H H O A E S T L A S B E S B
D O F T H E C O V E N A N T V
```

31

MANNA AND QUAIL FROM HEAVEN

EXODUS 16:4, 11–15

Then said the LORD unto Moses, Behold, I will _ _ _ _ bread from _ _ _ _ _ _ for you; and the people shall go out and gather a certain rate _ _ _ _ _ _ _ _ (2w), that I may prove them, whether they will walk in _ _ _ _ _ (2w), or no. . . . **11** And the LORD spake unto _ _ _ _ _, saying, **12** I have heard the _ _ _ _ _ _ _ _ _ _ of the children of _ _ _ _ _ _: speak unto them, saying, At even ye shall eat _ _ _ _ _, and in the morning ye shall be filled with _ _ _ _ _; and ye shall know that I am the _ _ _ _ your God. **13** And it _ _ _ _ _ _ _ _ _ _ _ (3w), that at even the _ _ _ _ _ _ _ came up, and covered the _ _ _ _: and in the morning the dew lay round about the host. **14** And when the _ _ _ that lay was gone up, _ _ _ _ _ _ _, upon the face of the _ _ _ _ _ _ _ _ _ _ _ there lay a small round thing, as small as the hoar frost on the ground. **15** And when the _ _ _ _ _ _ _ _ of Israel saw it, they said one to _ _ _ _ _ _ _, It is _ _ _ _ _: for they wist not what it was. And Moses said unto them, This is the bread which the LORD hath given you to _ _ _.

```
C V T E V E R Y D A Y M C C K
A N H A C K T S E O U E A L B
M O S E S H R Q W A L Y M T T
P A C R A L I H Z K T U E H O
L W H A T V I L I L R O T N I
N I A W T G E A D M S R O F E
J L L H X H S N U R R J P R M
S D N N W A Y R B Q E E A A S
G E R I D T I O O U W N S I S
B R E A D N B E H O L D S N H
K N H T G H I S L L M R T I P
Y E T S S O S P Y O A O A M O
N S O A L J A E S E N L C L W
O S N U P O Y N L H N R L R T
B D A W T I T O L F A E G D E
```

32

ELIJAH AND THE WIDOW

1 KINGS 17:7–16

And it came to pass after a while, that the _ _ _ _ _ dried up, because there had been no rain in the _ _ _ _. **8** And the _ _ _ _ _ _ _ _ _ _ _ _ (4w) came unto [Elijah], saying, **9** Arise, get thee to Zarephath, which belongeth to Zidon, and dwell there: behold, I have commanded a _ _ _ _ _ woman there to sustain thee. **10** So he arose and went to _ _ _ _ _ _ _ _ _. And when he came to the gate of the city, behold, the widow _ _ _ _ _ was there gathering of _ _ _ _ _ _: and he called to her, and said, Fetch me, I pray thee, a little water in a _ _ _ _ _ _, that I may _ _ _ _ _. **11** And as she was going to _ _ _ _ _ it, he called to her, and said, Bring me, I pray thee, a morsel of _ _ _ _ _ in thine hand. **12** And she said, As the LORD thy God liveth, I have not a cake, but an _ _ _ _ _ _ _ of meal in a barrel, and a little _ _ _ in a cruse: and, behold, I am gathering two sticks, that I may go in and dress it for me and my son, that we may eat it, and die. **13** And _ _ _ _ _ _ said unto her, _ _ _ _ _ _ _ (2w); go and do as thou hast said: but make me thereof a little _ _ _ _ first, and bring it unto me, and after make for thee and for thy son. **14** For thus saith the LORD God of _ _ _ _ _ _, The _ _ _ _ _ _ of meal shall not waste, neither shall the _ _ _ _ _ of oil fail, until the day that the LORD sendeth _ _ _ _ upon the earth. **15** And she went and did according to the saying of Elijah: and she, and he, and her _ _ _ _ _ _, did eat many days. **16** And the barrel of meal _ _ _ _ _ _ _ _ _ _ (2w), neither did the cruse of oil fail, according to the word of the LORD, which he spake by Elijah.

```
A M D R O L E H T F O D R O W
L L N S S N T A C H K Y H M A
L A A S T K O N S R P S O M S
N W L O I O N D A H O C K R T
K U F H C T E F K D U Z C A E
N M C A K E S U E O A C L S D
I R P I S E U L L R O H U I N
R H L H E L O A E H Y R N D O
D N N S G I H P S A C O B W T
A R S Y E J H B A M R Q U T O
E H N K N A D A N C E S W H N
R S L T T H L R W A K H I B R
B N N H P P F R D U M A D N A
A O N G T O O E N O R O O D E
A G V E S S E L R A I N W P F
```

33

JONAH

JONAH 2

Then Jonah prayed unto the LORD his God out of the fish's _ _ _ _ _, **2** And said, I cried by reason of mine _ _ _ _ _ _ _ _ _ _ unto the LORD, and he heard me; out of the belly of hell cried I, and thou heardest my voice. **3** For thou hadst cast me _ _ _ _   _ _ _   _ _ _ _ (3w), in the midst of the seas; and the _ _ _ _ _ _ compassed me about: all thy billows and thy _ _ _ _ _ passed over me. **4** Then I said, I am cast out of thy _ _ _ _ _; yet I will look again toward thy _ _ _ _   _ _ _ _ _ _ (2w). **5** The waters compassed me about, even to the soul: the _ _ _ _ _ closed me round about, the _ _ _ _ _ were wrapped about my head. **6** I went down to the bottoms of the _ _ _ _ _ _ _ _ _; the earth with her bars was about me for ever: yet hast thou brought up my life from corruption, _   _ _ _ _   _ _   _ _ _ (4w). **7** When my soul _ _ _ _ _ _ _ within me I _ _ _ _ _ _ _ _ _ _ the LORD: and my _ _ _ _ _ _ came in unto thee, into thine holy temple. **8** They that observe lying _ _ _ _ _ _ _ _ forsake their own _ _ _ _ _ _. **9** But I will sacrifice unto thee with the voice of _ _ _ _ _ _ _ _ _ _ _ _ _; I will pay that that I have vowed. _ _ _ _ _ _ _ _ _ _ is of the LORD. **10** And the LORD spake unto the fish, and it _ _ _ _ _ _ _ out Jonah upon the _ _ _ _ _ _ _ (2w).

```
O L A E W R L B S D E E W S N
S A L V A T I O N E N N P E O
E F E N V I O S R R M I S I I
I F P C E U N N A E B L E L V
T L H H S L L I R B E P S P O
I I N T Q U S C G M L P D E M
N C C P R A Y E R E L E O E I
A T A E O L O R D M Y G O D T
V I D D H O L Y T E M P L E E
I O R P S D N S A R O O F H D
N N Y P F A I N T E D C H T V
G B L G O G S N I A T N U O M
T B A K H N V A D V A G A T I
E L N T H A N K S G I V I N G
O A D R T C K Q U S R K E I N
```

34

THE GOOD SAMARITAN
LUKE 10:25-37

And, behold, a certain _ _ _ _ _ _ stood up, and tempted him, saying, Master, what shall I do to inherit eternal life? **26** He said unto him, What is written in the _ _ _? how readest thou? **27** And he answering said, Thou shalt _ _ _ _ the Lord thy God with all thy heart, and with all thy soul, and with all thy _ _ _ _ _ _ _ _, and with all thy mind; and thy neighbour as thyself. **28** And he said unto him, Thou hast _ _ _ _ _ _ _ _ right: this do, and thou shalt live. **29** But he, willing to justify himself, said unto Jesus, And who is my neighbour? **30** And Jesus answering said, A certain man went down from Jerusalem to _ _ _ _ _ _ _, and fell among thieves, which stripped him of his raiment, and wounded him, and departed, leaving him half _ _ _ _. **31** And by chance there came down a certain _ _ _ _ _ _ that way: and when he saw him, he passed by on the _ _ _ _ _ side. **32** And likewise a _ _ _ _ _ _ _, when he was at the place, came and looked on him, and passed by on the other side. **33** But a certain _ _ _ _ _ _ _ _ _ _, as he journeyed, came where he was: and when he saw him, he had compassion on him, **34** And went to him, and bound up his _ _ _ _ _ _, pouring in oil and wine, and set him on his own _ _ _ _ _, and brought him to an _ _ _, and took _ _ _ _ of him. **35** And on the morrow when he departed, he took out two pence, and gave them to the _ _ _ _, and said unto him, Take care of him; and whatsoever thou spendest more, when I come again, I will _ _ _ _ _ thee. **36** Which now of these three, thinkest thou, was neighbour unto him that

```
O T Y A P E R L L B A R A K E
N A T I R A M A S R E E S I S
U N S P I Z B V E D O N I B O
K S T R E N G T H E N O K W P
E W V L S I O L Q U K U N N X
T E O K T S W P P E M R O E V
H R T U M X L A W Y E R H W E
J E R I C H O I S L R T A S K
O D E A D E V A K M C L O T E
M N R I Z R E P R E Y O M H A
D E S E T L S H N F W D E I V
N A I V H L D C L E V I T E M
P A U U O T Y X N K L N S V L
O T S Q S G O I E P T N Z E A
O X A K T B B N N L B E A S T
```

fell among the _ _ _ _ _ _ _? **37** And he said, He that shewed _ _ _ _ _ _
on him. Then said Jesus unto him, Go, and do thou _ _ _ _ _ _ _ _.

35

PARABLE OF THE SOWER
MATTHEW 13:3-9, 18-23

Behold, a sower went forth to sow; **4** And when he _ _ _ _ _, some seeds fell by the way side, and the _ _ _ _ _ came and devoured them up: **5** Some fell upon _ _ _ _ _ _ _ _ _ _ _ (2w), where they had not much earth: and forthwith they _ _ _ _ _ _ _ _ _ (2w), because they had no deepness of _ _ _ _ _: **6** And when the sun was up, they were _ _ _ _ _ _ _ _ _; and because they had no root, they _ _ _ _ _ _ _ _ _ away. **7** And some fell among thorns; and the thorns sprung up, and _ _ _ _ _ _ _ them: **8** But other fell into good _ _ _ _ _ _, and brought forth _ _ _ _ _, some an hundredfold, some sixtyfold, some thirtyfold. **9** Who hath ears to hear, let him hear. . . . **18** Hear ye therefore the parable of the sower. **19** When any one heareth the word of the _ _ _ _ _ _ _, and understandeth it not, then cometh the _ _ _ _ _ _ _ _ _ (2w), and catcheth away that which was sown in his heart. This is he which received _ _ _ _ by the way side. **20** But he that received the seed into stony places, the same is he that heareth the word, and anon with _ _ _ receiveth it; **21** Yet hath he not _ _ _ _ in himself, but dureth for a while: for when _ _ _ _ _ _ _ _ _ _ _ or persecution ariseth because of the word, by and by he is _ _ _ _ _ _ _ _. **22** He also that received seed among the thorns is he that heareth the word; and the care of this world, and the deceitfulness of _ _ _ _ _ _, choke the word, and he becometh _ _ _ _ _ _ _ _ _. **23** But he that received seed into the good ground is he that heareth the word, and understandeth it; which also beareth fruit, and bringeth forth, some an _ _ _ _ _ _ _ _ _ _ _, some sixty, some thirty.

```
W I T H E R E D E H C R O C S
S I R O P S C H O K E D T H S
L T I N G G S L W O F K O H E
U S E R I O D E D N E F F O C
F P K I S H E H W O F V G I A
T R I B U L A T I O N S H J L
I U O S S L R P C V F G N N P
U N J O Y J T P K R R R M R Y
R G S W T A H N E K H O U R N
F U H E S M M Y D C D U T I O
N P C D E E S S O G G N H C T
U U L W S S I H N R L D W H S
I F P B E O R I E B E L S E E
G J V N N O K Y V A P P V S R
H U N D R E D F O L D T I O N
```

36

PARABLE OF THE PRODIGAL SON
LUKE 15:11–24

11 And he said, A certain man had _ _ _   _ _ _ _ (2w): **12** And the younger of them said to his father, _ _ _ _ _ _, give me the portion of goods that falleth to me. And he divided unto them his living. **13** And not many days after the _ _ _ _ _ _ _ son gathered all together, and took his _ _ _ _ _ _ _ into a far country, and there wasted his substance with _ _ _ _ _ _ _ _ _ _ _ _ _ (2w). **14** And when he had spent all, there arose a mighty _ _ _ _ _ _ in that land; and he began to _ _ _ _ _ _ _ _ (3w). **15** And he went and joined himself to a citizen of that country; and he sent him into his fields to feed _ _ _ _ _. **16** And he would fain have filled his _ _ _ _ _ with the husks that the swine did eat: and no man gave unto him. **17** And when he came to himself, he said, How many hired _ _ _ _ _ _ _ _ of my father's have bread enough and to spare, and I perish with _ _ _ _ _ _! **18** I will arise and go to my father, and will say unto him, Father, I have sinned against _ _ _ _ _ _, and before thee, **19** And am no more worthy to be called thy son: make me as one of thy _ _ _ _ _ servants. **20** And he arose, and came to his father. But when he was yet a great way off, his father saw him, and had _ _ _ _ _ _ _ _ _ _, and ran, and fell on his neck, and _ _ _ _ _ _ _ him. **21** And the son said unto him, Father, I have sinned against heaven, and in thy sight, and am no more worthy to be _ _ _ _ _ _ _ _ _ _ _ _ (3w). **22** But the father said to his servants, Bring forth the best _ _ _ _ _, and put it on him; and put a _ _ _ _ _ on his hand, and shoes on his _ _ _ _ _: **23** And bring hither

```
G R E H T A F L A C T F O J N
D J O U R N E Y O U N G E R N
B L R O L S E A R T H N M O C
P S A C M S T N A W N I E B E
I P M A O V C E J O F V R E R
Y H B L B M K B R S R I R E V
I R P L M H P E M O U L Y O D
T H T E J E G A U N L S Q U E
F E W D E N H H S S L U S B S
E P O T U T P E R S F O S B S
N H S H E A V E N N I T W A I
I N L Y L L E B J P P O I O K
M A I S E R V A N T S I N L P
A E R O A J O I G N I R E L E
F O U N D L P C E Y H C U Y R
```

the fatted _ _ _ _, and kill it; and let us eat, and be _ _ _ _ _ _: **24** For this my son was dead, and is alive again; he was lost, and is _ _ _ _ _. And they began to be merry.

37

JESUS HEALS MANY

LUKE 8:43–48; 17:11–19

And a woman having an _ _ _ _ _ _ _ _ _ _ _ _ (3w) twelve years, which had spent all her living upon _ _ _ _ _ _ _ _ _ _, neither could be healed of any, **44** Came behind him, and touched the border of his _ _ _ _ _ _ _: and immediately her issue of blood stanched. **45** And Jesus said, _ _ _ _ _ _ _ _ _ _ _ (3w)? When all denied, Peter and they that were with him said, _ _ _ _ _ _, the multitude throng thee and press thee, and sayest thou, Who touched me? **46** And Jesus said, _ _ _ _ _ _ _ _ hath touched me: for I perceive that _ _ _ _ _ _ is gone out of me. **47** And when the _ _ _ _ _ saw that she was not hid, she came _ _ _ _ _ _ _ _ _, and falling down before him, she declared unto him before all the people for what cause she had touched him, and how she was _ _ _ _ _ _ immediately. **48** And he said unto her, _ _ _ _ _ _ _ _, be of good comfort: thy faith hath made thee whole; go in peace.

And it came to pass, as he went to Jerusalem, that he passed through the midst of Samaria and _ _ _ _ _ _ _. **12** And as he entered into a certain village, there met him ten men that were _ _ _ _ _ _ _, which stood afar off: **13** And they lifted up their _ _ _ _ _ _, and said, Jesus, Master, have _ _ _ _ _ on us. **14** And when he saw them, he said unto them, Go shew yourselves unto the _ _ _ _ _ _ _. And it came to pass, that, as they went, they were _ _ _ _ _ _ _ _ _. **15** And one of them, when he saw that he was healed, turned back, and with a loud voice glorified God, **16** And fell down on his face at his feet, giving him thanks: and he was a Samaritan.

```
C A T G N I L B M E R T H V O
H K S O M E B O D Y S G E Y L
C E N R A I E S C R S W L E G
L S A S N U T R N O C H O P T
E H I S T L E P N L H O H P S
A X C R L M S H O G V T W I T
N W I S S U E O F B L O O D R
S V S G G A R M E N T U M A A
E O Y Q M Y D E Q U J C A U N
D I H U M W E L T K C H N G G
E C P R I E S T S S K E N H E
L E P E R S C E P P A D G T R
A S T I O N I G N I Z M H E K
E O L J D D G A L I L E E R L
H T I A F V O M A X N N N J A
```

17 And Jesus answering said, Were there not ten cleansed? but where are the _ _ _ _? **18** There are not found that returned to give _ _ _ _ _ to God, save this _ _ _ _ _ _ _ _ _. **19** And he said unto him, Arise, go thy way: thy _ _ _ _ _ hath made thee _ _ _ _ _ _.

38

THE HOLY SPIRIT ARRIVES

ACTS 2:1-8, 12-21

And when the day of _ _ _ _ _ _ _ _ _ was fully come, they were all with one accord in one place. **2** And suddenly there came a sound from heaven as of a rushing _ _ _ _ _ _ _ _ _ _ (2w), and it filled all the house where they were sitting. **3** And there appeared unto them cloven tongues like as of _ _ _ _, and it sat upon each of them. **4** And they were all filled with the _ _ _ _ _ _ _ _ _ (2w), and began to speak with other _ _ _ _ _ _ _, as the Spirit gave them utterance. **5** And there were dwelling at Jerusalem Jews, devout men, out of every nation under _ _ _ _ _ _. **6** Now when this was noised abroad, the multitude came together, and were confounded, because that every man heard them speak in his own _ _ _ _ _ _ _ _. **7** And they were all amazed and marvelled, saying one to another, Behold, are not all these which speak Galilaeans? **8** And how hear we every man in our own tongue, wherein we were _ _ _ _? . . . **12** And they were all amazed, and were in _ _ _ _ _, saying one to another, What meaneth this? **13** Others _ _ _ _ _ _ _ said, These men are full of new wine. **14** But Peter, standing up with the _ _ _ _ _ _, lifted up his voice, and said unto them, Ye men of _ _ _ _ _ _, and all ye that dwell at Jerusalem, be this known unto you, and hearken to my words: **15** For these are not _ _ _ _ _ _ _, as ye suppose, seeing it is but the third hour of the day. **16** But this is that which was spoken by the prophet Joel; **17** And it shall come to pass in the _ _ _ _ _ _ _ _ (2w), saith God, I will pour out of my _ _ _ _ _ _ upon all flesh: and your sons and your daughters shall prophesy, and your young men shall see visions, and

```
E I T O N G U E S A C O S P L
A P L K E E E R K C P H S D S
N F D E V A S E B H S T R O N
E Y H R A F R M Y V S E T U D
V S A E E H L A A O G S H B G
E E N T H P G V C E O Y Y T O
L D D O O L B E L L R A S J O
E P M I G H T Y W I N D E U R
G F A L L N K B R O E T G D T
A F I R E E E E O T I S N A T
U Z D P T K Y M L R V A I E H
G Y E X O P P A I K N L K A A
N N N M N C K P R L G P C G G
A T S L P T S O H G Y L O H N
L K I D R U N K E N N N M H C
```

your old men shall dream _ _ _ _ _ _ _: **18** And on my servants and on my _ _ _ _ _ _ _ _ _ _ _ _ _ I will pour out in those days of my Spirit; and they shall prophesy: **19** And I will shew wonders in heaven above, and signs in the earth beneath; _ _ _ _ _ _, and fire, and vapour of _ _ _ _ _ _: **20** The sun shall be turned into darkness, and the _ _ _ _ _ into blood, before the great and notable day of the Lord come: **21** And it shall come to pass, that whosoever shall call on the name of the Lord shall _ _ _ _ _ _ _ (2w).

39

JESUS' BIRTH
LUKE 2:1-20

And it came to pass in those days, that there went out a _ _ _ _ _ _ from Caesar Augustus that all the world should be taxed. **2** (And this taxing was first made when Cyrenius was governor of Syria.) **3** And all went to be _ _ _ _ _, every one into his own city. **4** And _ _ _ _ _ _ also went up from Galilee, out of the city of _ _ _ _ _ _ _ _, into Judaea, unto the city of David, which is called Bethlehem; (because he was of the house and lineage of _ _ _ _ _:) **5** To be taxed with Mary his espoused wife, being great with _ _ _ _ _. **6** And so it was, that, while they were there, the days were accomplished that she should be delivered. **7** And she brought forth her _ _ _ _ _ _ _ _ _ son, and wrapped him in swaddling clothes, and laid him in a _ _ _ _ _ _; because there was no room for them in the _ _ _. **8** And there were in the same country shepherds abiding in the field, keeping watch over their _ _ _ _ _ by night. **9** And, lo, the angel of the Lord came upon them, and the glory of the Lord shone round about them: and they were sore _ _ _ _ _ _. **10** And the angel said unto them, _ _ _ _ _ _ _ (2w): for, behold, I bring you good tidings of great joy, which shall be to all _ _ _ _ _ _. **11** For unto you is born this day in the city of David a _ _ _ _ _ _ _, which is Christ the Lord. **12** And this shall be a sign unto you; Ye shall find the babe wrapped in swaddling _ _ _ _ _ _ _, lying in a manger. **13** And suddenly there was with the angel a multitude of the heavenly _ _ _ _ praising God, and saying, **14** _ _ _ _ _ to God in the highest, and on earth peace, good will toward men. **15** And it came to pass, as the angels were gone away from them into heaven, the shepherds said one to _ _ _ _ _ _ _ _, Let us now go even unto _ _ _ _ _ _ _ _ _, and see this thing which is come to pass, which

```
N L P E P R N H J M M S F I E
O A J O R D A V I D D S H N J
I E R K T P Z F N O L A T P G
T B E A S N A W R W N I O Z H
S A V I O U R K E A K Q H T K
N B E T H L E H E M I U U C T
N A Z F Y W T E L G O D O L S
S G W I J J H A L U G L E O F
F E A R N O T R X D F O S T H
R K O S X S R T A E H T G H P
L D I T R E E R C E D G L E P
O L N B L P A C Y S J O O S H
E A N O T H E R D H R P R A N
K I W R H W A L X D L T Y Z G
R E G N A M C H U E L H I C K
```

the Lord hath made known unto us. **16** And they came with haste, and found _ _ _ _, and Joseph, and the _ _ _ _ lying in a manger. **17** And when they had seen it, they made known abroad the saying which was told them concerning this child. **18** And all they that heard it wondered at those things which were told them by the shepherds. **19** But Mary kept all these things, and pondered them in her _ _ _ _ _. **20** And the shepherds returned, glorifying and praising _ _ _ for all the things that they had heard and seen, as it was _ _ _ _ unto them.

40

JESUS DEDICATED AT THE TEMPLE
LUKE 2:25-39

25 And, behold, there was a man in Jerusalem, whose name was _ _ _ _ _ _; and the same man was just and _ _ _ _ _ _, waiting for the consolation of Israel: and the _ _ _ _ _ _ _ _ (2w) was upon him. **26** And it was revealed unto him by the Holy Ghost, that he should not see death, before he had seen the Lord's _ _ _ _ _ _. **27** And he came by the Spirit into the temple: and when the _ _ _ _ _ _ _ brought in the child Jesus, to do for him after the custom of the _ _ _, **28** Then took he him up in his arms, and blessed God, and said, **29** Lord, now lettest thou thy servant depart in peace, according to thy word: **30** For mine eyes have seen thy _ _ _ _ _ _ _ _ _, **31** Which thou hast prepared before the face of all people; **32** A light to lighten the Gentiles, and the glory of thy people _ _ _ _ _ _. **33** And Joseph and his mother marvelled at those things which were spoken of him. **34** And Simeon blessed them, and said unto _ _ _ _ his mother, Behold, this _ _ _ _ _ is set for the fall and rising again of many in Israel; and for a sign which shall be spoken against; **35** (Yea, a sword shall pierce through thy own _ _ _ _ also,) that the thoughts of many hearts may be _ _ _ _ _ _ _ _. **36** And there was one _ _ _ _, a prophetess, the daughter of Phanuel, of the tribe of Aser: she was of a great age, and had lived with an _ _ _ _ _ _ _ seven years from her virginity; **37** And she was a _ _ _ _ _ of about fourscore and four years, which departed not from the _ _ _ _ _ _, but served God with fastings and _ _ _ _ _ _ _ night and day. **38** And she coming in that

```
N E L T I O N P K C J A C T H
L R C H I L D N A B S U H D O
E E I G G G L S H K W R R W L
H Q U L R Y K M N P S N I P Y
R F I I A N N A A P R N S H G
E Y S N S U H A Y R E D T K H
V D R M I T N G Z X Y E W E O
E N A Y M S N O I T A V L A S
A K E I E H P E L K R O S G T
L E L N O W P T R L P U D X H
E L L G N S I O E A J T D G S
D S E X K R E D E M P T I O N
R U A N M M C D O A P K U C E
R K E G L J L H T W A L K W R
Y E S A I O G A L I L E E P P
```

instant gave _ _ _ _ _ _ likewise unto the Lord, and spake of him to all them that looked for _ _ _ _ _ _ _ _ _ _ in Jerusalem. **39** And when they had performed all things according to the law of the Lord, they returned into _ _ _ _ _ _ _, to their own city Nazareth.

41

THE WISE MEN
MATTHEW 2:1-12

Now when Jesus was born in Bethlehem of _ _ _ _ _ _ in the days of _ _ _ _ _ the king, behold, there came wise men from the east to Jerusalem, **2** Saying, Where is he that is born _ _ _ _ _ _ _ _ _ _ _ _ (4w)? for we have seen his _ _ _ _ in the _ _ _ _, and are come to worship him. **3** When Herod the king had heard these things, he was _ _ _ _ _ _ _ _ _, and all Jerusalem with him. **4** And when he had gathered all the chief _ _ _ _ _ _ _ and scribes of the people together, he demanded of them where _ _ _ _ _ _ should be born. **5** And they said unto him, In Bethlehem of Judaea: for thus it is written by the _ _ _ _ _ _ _, **6** And thou Bethlehem, in the land of Juda, art not the least among the _ _ _ _ _ _ _ _ of Juda: for out of thee shall come a Governor, that shall _ _ _ _ my people Israel. **7** Then Herod, when he had privily called the _ _ _ _ _ _ _ (2w), enquired of them diligently what time the star appeared. **8** And he sent them to Bethlehem, and said, Go and search diligently for the young child; and when ye have found him, bring me word again, that I may come and _ _ _ _ _ _ _ _ him also. **9** When they had heard the king, they departed; and, lo, the star, which they saw in the east, went before them, till it came and stood over where the _ _ _ _ _ child was. **10** When they saw the star, they _ _ _ _ _ _ _ _ _ with exceeding great joy. **11** And when they were come into the _ _ _ _ _ _, they saw the young child with _ _ _ _ his mother, and fell down, and worshipped him: and when they had opened their _ _ _ _ _ _ _ _ _, they presented unto him

```
C A M Y R R H R E P M O O S A
T T W O R S H I P S P R I N P
S E R U S A E R T W R E Y V N
I H R N E E X A R E I P E O W
R P V G H I R R O J N K L N Y
H O U S E R B E U E C P G K G
C R A M A E R D B H E R O D R
H P M O D U A S L T S I L E O
N E R O L E V H E F J E D C Q
N W D E A U Y A D O R S T I U
A V D W T J R K N G Z T I O G
Q W N P P E A S T N T S O J M
U J E T N E M E S I W H N E M
R W M N N Y L E N K D P W R A
W Y I N G O N V N O H T J E R
```

gifts; _ _ _ _, and frankincense and _ _ _ _ _ _. **12** And being warned of God in a _ _ _ _ _ _ that they should not return to Herod, they departed into their own country another way.

42

JESUS TEACHES AT THE TEMPLE
LUKE 2:40-52

And the child _ _ _ _, and waxed strong in spirit, filled with _ _ _ _ _ _: and the grace of God was upon him. **41** Now his _ _ _ _ _ _ _ went to Jerusalem every year at the feast of the _ _ _ _ _ _ _ _. **42** And when he was _ _ _ _ _ _ years old, they went up to Jerusalem after the custom of the feast. **43** And when they had fulfilled the days, as they returned, the child Jesus tarried behind in Jerusalem; and _ _ _ _ _ _ and his mother knew not of it. **44** But they, supposing him to have been in the company, went a day's journey; and they sought him among their _ _ _ _ _ _ _ _ and acquaintance. **45** And when they found him not, they turned back again to _ _ _ _ _ _ _ _ _, seeking him. **46** And it _ _ _ _ _ _ _ _ _ _ (3w), that after three days they found him in the _ _ _ _ _ _, sitting in the midst of the doctors, both hearing them, and asking them questions. **47** And all that heard him were astonished at his _ _ _ _ _ _ _ _ _ _ _ _ _ _ and answers. **48** And when they saw him, they were _ _ _ _ _ _: and his mother said unto him, _ _ _, why hast thou thus dealt with us? behold, thy _ _ _ _ _ _ and I have sought thee sorrowing. **49** And he said unto them, How is it that ye sought me? wist ye not that I must be about my Father's _ _ _ _ _ _ _ _? **50** And they understood not the saying which he spake unto them. **51** And he went down with them, and came to _ _ _ _ _ _ _ _, and was subject unto them: but his _ _ _ _ _ _ kept all these sayings in her _ _ _ _ _. **52** And Jesus increased in wisdom and _ _ _ _ _ _ _ _, and in favour with God and _ _ _.

```
I P T A L I O N S H X N G P W
N E J E S S E N I S U B D L O
G T W E L V E M A R H D D J N
N P K I N S F O L K T H S E M
I A R T S P Q U L T E W E R G
D R V O E D I J C L R D J U E
N E N E Z N O H P J A P E S M
A N I L N S A M D E Z A M A D
T T W S E N E R X O A S O L D
S S A P O T E M A C N S M E V
R W H E A R T O E M P O L M E
E R E R U T A T S K E V T C H
D T P P X O F H A C U E L Z I
N A M L L K O E F L B R F R G
U B R E A N N R E H T A F A H
```

43

JESUS TURNS WATER INTO WINE
JOHN 2:1-11

And the third day there was a _ _ _ _ _ _ _ _ in Cana of Galilee; and the mother of Jesus was there: **2** And both _ _ _ _ _ was called, and his disciples, to the marriage. **3** And when they wanted _ _ _ _, the _ _ _ _ _ _ of Jesus saith unto him, They have no wine. **4** Jesus saith unto her, _ _ _ _ _, what have I to do with thee? mine hour is not yet come. **5** His mother saith unto the servants, Whatsoever he saith unto you, _ _ _ _ (2w). **6** And there were set there _ _ _ waterpots of _ _ _ _ _, after the manner of the _ _ _ _ _ _ _ _ _ of the Jews, containing two or three firkins apiece. **7** Jesus saith unto them, Fill the waterpots with _ _ _ _ _. And they filled them up to the _ _ _ _. **8** And he saith unto them, Draw out now, and bear unto the governor of the _ _ _ _ _. And they bare it. **9** When the _ _ _ _ _ of the feast had tasted the water that was made wine, and knew not whence it was: (but the _ _ _ _ _ _ _ _ which drew the water knew;) the _ _ _ _ _ _ _ _ of the feast called the bridegroom, **10** And saith unto him, Every man at the beginning doth set forth good wine; and when men have well _ _ _ _ _, then that which is worse: but thou hast kept the good wine until now. **11** This beginning of _ _ _ _ _ _ _ _ did Jesus in _ _ _ _ of Galilee, and manifested forth his _ _ _ _ _; and his disciples _ _ _ _ _ _ _ _ on him.

```
P I N R A L A W E E J U P A Y
L W C Y W I J Z K R E L U R J
L B E L I E V E D E A Y R E L
R X M B S N Q W E N E E I B X
G M K U O I Y U A E H O F Y U
Y C S E X W D C R T J O Y B E
S S T I C H O G O W E B I I E
Y R O L G T I M I S H R N N K
I J N I I Y T A A T Q I G G F
N F E A S T N R C N U M K O W
G L L E X N S R E A R N T O T
E C H S K A J I H V U S C K I
K R E H W C H A X R T H B T O
R O N R E V O G D E Z B J Y N
W M I R A C L E S S W O U O H
```

44

JESUS CALLS SIMON PETER

LUKE 5:1-11

And it came to pass, that, as the people pressed upon him to hear the
_ _ _ _ _ _ _ _ _ (3w), he stood by the lake of Gennesaret, **2** And saw
two _ _ _ _ _ standing by the lake: but the fishermen were gone out of
them, and were washing their _ _ _ _. **3** And he entered into one of the
ships, which was Simon's, and _ _ _ _ _ _ him that he would thrust out
a little from the land. And he sat down, and _ _ _ _ _ _ the people out
of the ship. **4** Now when he had left speaking, he said unto _ _ _ _ _,
Launch out into the _ _ _ _, and let down your nets for a draught.
5 And Simon answering said unto him, _ _ _ _ _ _, we have toiled all
the night, and have taken _ _ _ _ _ _ _: nevertheless at thy word I will
let down the net. **6** And when they had this done, they inclosed a great
multitude of _ _ _ _ _ _: and their net brake. **7** And they beckoned unto
their partners, which were in the other ship, that they should come and
_ _ _ _ them. And they came, and _ _ _ _ _ _ both the ships, so that they
began to _ _ _ _. **8** When Simon _ _ _ _ _ _ saw it, he fell down at Jesus'
knees, saying, Depart from me; for I am a sinful man, _ _ _ _ _ (2w).
9 For he was astonished, and all that were with him, at the draught of
the fishes which they had taken: **10** And so was also James, and _ _ _ _ _,
the sons of Zebedee, which were partners with Simon. And _ _ _ _ _ _ said
unto Simon, _ _ _ _ _ _ _ (2w); from henceforth thou shalt catch _ _ _.
11 And when they had brought their ships to _ _ _ _, they forsook all,
and _ _ _ _ _ _ _ _ him.

```
L M L A N D E W O L L O F O L
E S I S W R E O X E D A E P H
B J H S B P V R E T E P A B D
I R F I L L E D C R E W R R O
K E G N I H T O N E P O N L O
A O F K N G S F S S I M O N J
Y P N O O U I G W G A R T T I
T L H Z S H K O N S D M A M Y
I X O E Z T E D H M W E U E E
O A J W O A E N E M A L G L M
N M S P M Y M N L F I S H E S
P I H A A R J A P O Q U T D K
N G I R O N Y U S B S I A E C
Z A P S T O L L C O E J T E R
E K S O Y I N G K O T U N N I
```

45

ZACCHAEUS
LUKE 19:2–10

And, behold, there was a man named Zacchaeus, which was the _ _ _ _ _ among the _ _ _ _ _ _ _ _ _, and he was _ _ _ _. **3** And he sought to see Jesus who he was; and could not for the press, because he was _ _ _ _ _ _ of stature. **4** And he ran before, and _ _ _ _ _ _ _ _ up into a _ _ _ _ _ _ _ _ _ tree to see him: for he was to pass that way. **5** And when _ _ _ _ _ came to the place, he looked up, and saw him, and said unto him, Zacchaeus, make _ _ _ _ _, and come down; for to day I must abide at thy _ _ _ _ _. **6** And he made haste, and came down, and received him _ _ _ _ _ _ _ _. **7** And when they saw it, they all _ _ _ _ _ _ _ _, saying, That he was gone to be guest with a man that is a _ _ _ _ _ _. **8** And Zacchaeus stood, and said unto the Lord: Behold, Lord, the half of my goods I give to the _ _ _ _; and if I have taken any thing from any man by _ _ _ _ _ accusation, I restore him _ _ _ _ _ _ _ _. **9** And Jesus said unto him, This day is _ _ _ _ _ _ _ _ _ come to this house, forsomuch as he also is a _ _ _ of _ _ _ _ _ _ _. **10** For the Son of man is come to _ _ _ _ and to _ _ _ _ that which was _ _ _ _.

```
O Y E S U O H A L C H J E V E
R M A J N R C L I M B E D C K
G O S O N L I N T E A S A U C
C R R Y G E R Y T H D U M G H
A N I F C S T O L S W S M A N
J A E U E O X Q E D O A U S U
N R V L R U M U L A H L R T P
N E S L A F O O S A L V M E K
F N P Y I B F R R K O A U R E
A N R O J R B B O E O T R S I
R I A N U R A E O C H I E F P
E S T O E H T T P S T O D O P
N T F E P U B L I C A N S T D
M E S G O S S A L A I N G C R
H A S T E V A S E E K F E A Y
```

46

PAUL AND SILAS IN PRISON
ACTS 16:25-36

And at _ _ _ _ _ _ _ _ _ Paul and Silas prayed, and _ _ _ _ praises unto God: and the prisoners heard them. **26** And suddenly there was a great _ _ _ _ _ _ _ _ _ _, so that the foundations of the prison were shaken: and immediately all the _ _ _ _ _ were opened, and every one's bands were loosed. **27** And the keeper of the _ _ _ _ _ _ awaking out of his _ _ _ _ _, and seeing the prison doors _ _ _ _ _, he drew out his _ _ _ _ _, and would have killed himself, supposing that the _ _ _ _ _ _ _ _ _ had been fled. **28** But Paul cried with a loud voice, saying, Do thyself no _ _ _ _: for we are all here. **29** Then he called for a light, and sprang in, and came _ _ _ _ _ _ _ _ _, and fell down before Paul and Silas, **30** And brought them out, and said, Sirs, what must I do to be _ _ _ _ _? **31** And they said, Believe on the Lord Jesus _ _ _ _ _ _, and thou shalt be saved, and thy _ _ _ _ _ _. **32** And they spake unto him the word of the Lord, and to all that were in his house. **33** And he took them the same hour of the _ _ _ _ _, and washed their stripes; and was _ _ _ _ _ _ _ _, he and all his, straightway. **34** And when he had brought them into his house, he set _ _ _ _ before them, and rejoiced, believing in _ _ _ with all his house. **35** And when it was day, the magistrates sent the serjeants, saying, Let those men go. **36** And the _ _ _ _ _ _ of the prison told this saying to Paul, The magistrates have sent to let you go: now therefore depart, and go in _ _ _ _ _.

```
T O N J E I O M A K N C S W B
S K S W T D P R I S O N C J U
I D S D A E E D A B O T P L K
A C L K E Y N N O Y Q R E S C
G W A L M V G J X U I E A P S
A R S H C A H W S K M C A T N
N T T D R O W S O A N B E H H
R E P E E K R N U B N L G A G
A H O Z Q C E Q J B S I R R I
N K N I U R H I E Y N N U M N
D E C T S T O R N K E G P G D
D J K P R S U N I G N X O O I
T Y F A A W S N R S O M O D M
E R E B S T E G K D T R C H A
A J E M M H P P A E S T I O N
```

JESUS RAISES LAZARUS FROM THE DEAD

JOHN 11:20-27, 32-35, 41-44

Then Martha, as soon as she heard that Jesus was coming, went and met him: but Mary sat still in the house. **21** Then said _ _ _ _ _ _ unto Jesus, Lord, if thou hadst been here, my brother had not died. **22** But I know, that even now, whatsoever thou wilt ask of _ _ _, God will give it thee. **23** Jesus saith unto her, Thy _ _ _ _ _ _ _ shall rise again. **24** Martha saith unto him, I know that he shall _ _ _ _ again in the resurrection at the last _ _ _. **25** Jesus said unto her, I am the _ _ _ _ _ _ _ _ _ _ _ _ _, and the life: he that believeth in me, though he were _ _ _ _, yet shall he live: **26** And whosoever liveth and believeth in me shall never die. Believest thou this? **27** She saith unto him, Yea, Lord: I believe that thou art the _ _ _ _ _ _, the Son of God, which should come into the _ _ _ _ _. . . . **32** Then when Mary was come where Jesus was, and saw him, she fell down at his _ _ _ _, saying unto him, Lord, if thou hadst been here, my brother had not _ _ _ _. **33** When Jesus therefore saw her weeping, and the Jews also _ _ _ _ _ _ _ _ which came with her, he groaned in the _ _ _ _ _ _, and was troubled. **34** And said, Where have ye laid him? They said unto him, Lord, come and see. **35** Jesus _ _ _ _. . . . **41** Then they took away the _ _ _ _ _ from the place where the dead was laid. And Jesus lifted up his eyes, and said, Father, I thank thee that thou hast _ _ _ _ _ _ me. **42** And I knew that thou hearest me always: but because of the people which stand by I said it, that they may believe that thou hast

```
I L A S T G C D Y D U O G E X
N U F A H R H M B R O T H E R
D Y H T E B R O D E T I I S E
E G E E Q R I H L A Z A R U S
C Z L E U E S I R F H H S P U
S L R F N N T Y O H Y T I T R
T L A G A O O X W T P R Y E R
A E I X U C N E O R I A D Y E
O H U Q U O E S L T D M H O C
N N V H O P D E L S H W E P T
E Y E A I A M R T G C J A G I
X R R N E E H D I O Z C R N O
A C G D E A D M O D E I D I N
A L U D R E Y M N V B H T Z R
T H O M O S S R H O M E P P H
```

sent me. **43** And when he thus had spoken, he cried with a loud voice, _ _ _ _ _ _ _, come forth. **44** And he that was dead came forth, bound _ _ _ _ and foot with graveclothes: and his _ _ _ _ was bound about with a napkin. Jesus saith unto them, Loose him, and let him go.

ANSWERS

1

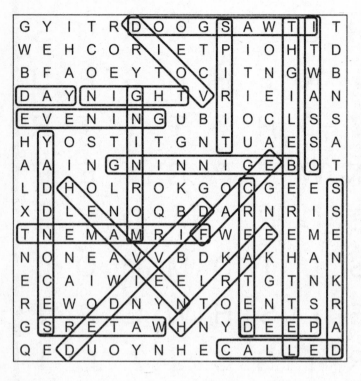

2

3

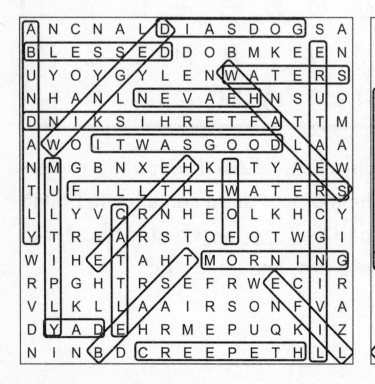

4

ANSWERS

5

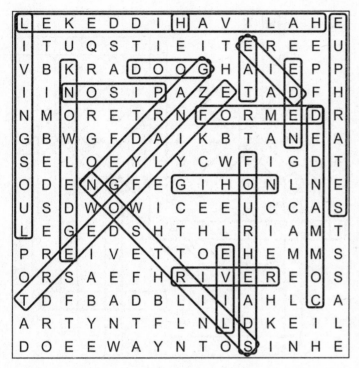

6

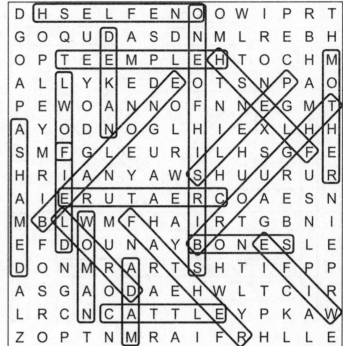

7

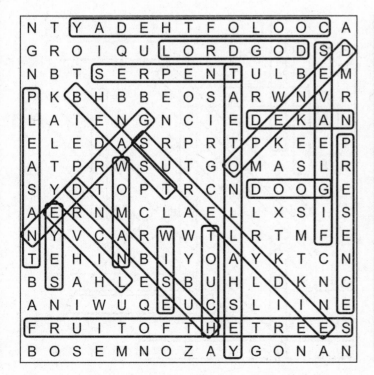

8

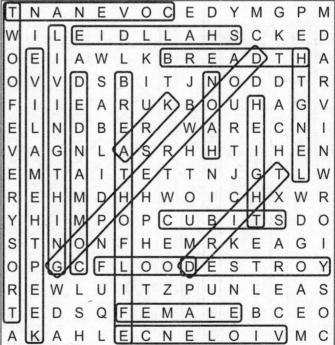

ANSWERS

9

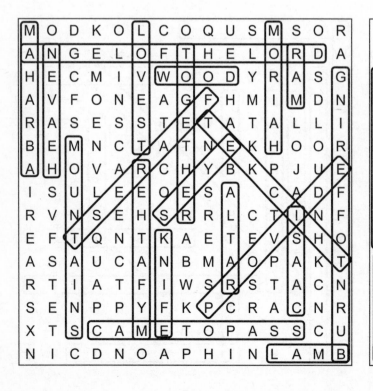

10

```
L O O E S R U C R O U L S T U
O D G S N O A H O W A L T A R
V M H D O I T O K F I R K B E
M A N T S E V R A H N I W K T
U C R H R Q U J Y D E R R S N
L E A G A A K G N I A A S E I
T K T I Z P E K D S E G T V W
I A S N Y P W O T H C D E I B
P P R U O V A S T E E W S N G
L S G N I R E F F O T N R U B
Y M P H H A O O R B O L W W R
O I N O I T A N I G A M I D E
R T H T U O Y E E C H R F C E
R E S O H T E P E E R C E N D
B X S N I R P T Z O M Y S X O
```

10

```
H E O M N L F A M I L I E S M
S L M A C L O I S E T I N E K
R L D R I B R M E X E K T T Z
E E T B S H B W T P S S T I Z
P C H A S L K E A L Y A R S E
H Z I O E D N S R O A E T U S
A T S D I B G Z P D A I D E C
I D E P Z G E Z U N M U S J O
S E T I Z Z I N E K O B E N U
R H I S I A H V D J R I S E T
O I T T R L O C H E I F U S R
H G T C E C G O N A T I O N Y
C R I K P Z D M A S E T H S L
M W H T E S R U C B S T G H S
```

11

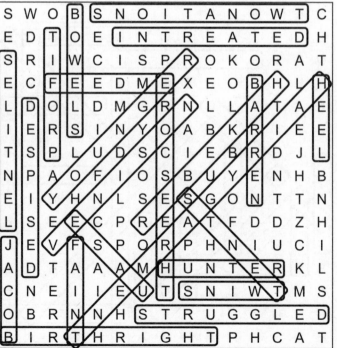

12

```
S W O B S N O I T A N O W T C
E D T O E I N T R E A T E D H
S R I W C I S P R O K O R A T
E C W F E E D M E X E O B H L
L I D O L D M G R N L L A T E
I E R S I N Y O A B K R I E L
T P A O F I O S B U Y E N H B
N I Y H N L S E S G O N T N
E S E E C P R E A T F D Z H
L J E V F S P O R P H N I U C I
A D T A A M H U N T E R K L
C N E I I E U T S N I W T M S
O B R N N H S T R U G G L E D
B I R T H R I G H T P H C A T
```

ANSWERS

13

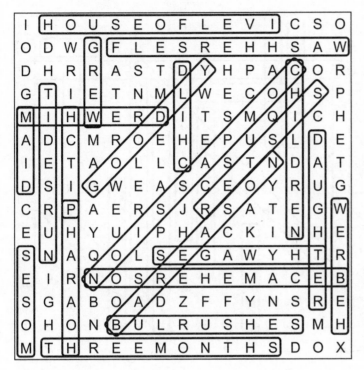

```
I H O U S E O F L E V I C S O
O D W G F L E S R E H H S A W
D H R R A S T D Y H P A C O R
G T I E T N M L W E C O H S P
M I H W E R D I T S M Q I C H
A D C M R O E H E P U S L D E
I E T A O L L C A S T N D A T
D S I G W E A S C E O Y R U G
C R P A E R S J R S A T E G W
E U H Y U I P H A C K I N H E
S N A Q O L S E G A W Y H T R
S G I R N O S R E H E M A C E B
O H O B O A D Z F F Y N S R E
M T H R E E M O N T H S D O X
```

14

```
S O R B O U B M O U N T A I N
P K A S D C U A L T L U R A O
T C E A T U S L M I D I A N I T
A O F F A T H E R I N L A W T
C N O I L E E T S M U E O R C I
A S S S H O E S P H O Y R K I
N U W T H E C S N Y R W O I L
A M O S E S C K E L G E C A F
N E R N A Q U H S L Y E E W F
I D R O L E H T F O L E G N A
T B O G G D A J B B O W X A B
I C S M I L K A N D H O N E Y
E O E L O X D C A A S I S T A
S R T G H C C O R B A U Z I Y
L L B W A K A B R A H A M A N
```

15

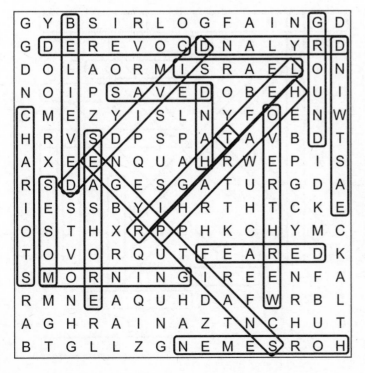

```
G Y B S I R L O G F A I N G D
G D E R E V O C D N A L Y R D
D O L A O R M I S R A E L O N
N O I P S A V E D O B E H U I
C M E Z Y I S L N Y F O E N W
H R V S D P S P A T A V B D T
A X E E N Q U A H R W E P I S
R I S D A G E S G A T U R G D A
I O E S S B Y I H R T H T C K E
O T S T H X R P P H K C H Y M C
T S O V O R Q U T F E A R E D
S M O R N I N G I R E E N F A
R M N E A Q U H D A F W R B L
A G H R A I N A Z T N C H U T
B T G L L Z G N E M E S R O H
```

16

```
E D E I L N V E R E W D Z N G
C H R C U S S H I L O H H R S
D I K D E L A E V E R U S B O
E T M D A S T L M I D X A W N
V R L A Y D O W N T O N R A O
I S R A E L G O H O F S O N D
E S S P L R Y F U B T T S L L
C E B N E O E T Q Y H P E E X
R R S W A B E H S R E E B E T
E V A E N M U I L A L L R I U
P A M S P D D R K A O G L D A
N U L T T O D M O R N D F L
Z T E H P O R P P I D I N E S
F I L A P T H E A R E T H O G
N G A M D A U L T H G T D N E
```

ANSWERS

17

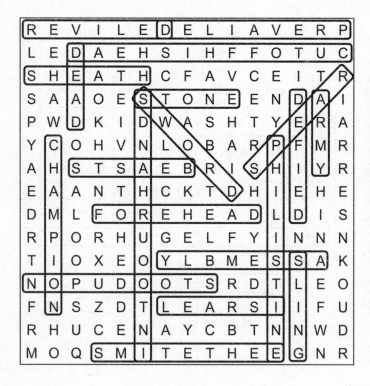

18

R E V I L E D E L I A V E R P
L E D A E H S I H F F O T U C
S H E A T H C F A V C E I T R
S A A O E S T O N E E N D A I
P W D K I D W A S H T Y E R A
Y A C O H V N L O B A R P F M R
A H S T S A E B R I S H I Y E
E A A N T H C K T D H I E H E
D M L F O R E H E A D L D I S
R P O R H U G E L F Y I N N N
T I O X E O Y L B M E S S A K
N O P U D O O T S R D T L E O
F N S Z D T L E A R S I I F U
R H U C E N A Y C B T N N W D
M O Q S M I T E T H E E G N R

I A P S F E N R G N I T S A F
E R A I N S T R U M E N T S R
D A L G Y L G N I D E E C X E
E T A N G E L O E E K B O K V
N B C E J O G D E L U Q N I E
O C E T E P N A L I G L T V R
F R A C R A I R B V U N I H O
L A U I M H N I A E P W N A F
I T H M T R R U T R E Z U D E
O E O S S T O S N T R Z A J V
N C D T T H M A E H S N L I L
S H T U O M W R M E I E L P U
S Y S I N I T X A E A A Y U C
G O S R E P R O L F N B D E T
M D O C R D E R E P S O R P N

19

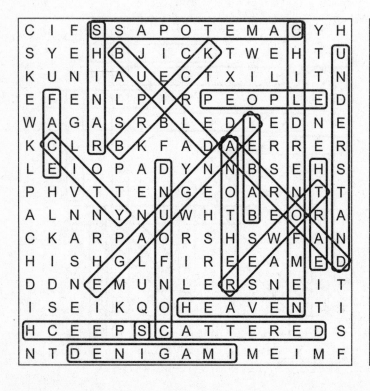

20

C I F S S A P O T E M A C Y H
S Y E H B J I C K T W E H T U
K U N I A U E C T X I L I T N
E F E N L P I R P E O P L E D
W A G A S R B L E D L E D N E
K C L R B K F A D A E R R E R
L E I O P A D Y N N B S E H S
P H V T T E N G E O A R N T T
A L N N Y N U W H T B E O R A
C K A R P A O R S H S W F A N
H I S H G L F I R E E A M E D
D D N E M U N L E R S N E I T
I S E I K Q O H E A V E N T I
H C E E P S C A T T E R E D S
N T D E N I G A M I M E I M F

G N I D N E C S E D E W O V N
A K N P E R T E N T H E U Q R
C T A E O T D A E R B B T
W A H C B A E I H E A V E N T
P E I R G R W T D S F R E Y Z
H R S P S B A D E M A E R D
C A P T O R A H C N H A S O Y
N Y L C D L A I A T E Q H G G
E E A S T G E L H M C U E N E
R J C L H A P T L R A I B M A
S L E E P H I N F I E E A E S
D B Z G S W O L L I P A C B S
E E C N M R I C A A S I O P U
G E K A X T E E A S S R Y W M
L L I E G E R N B E T H E L B

ANSWERS

21

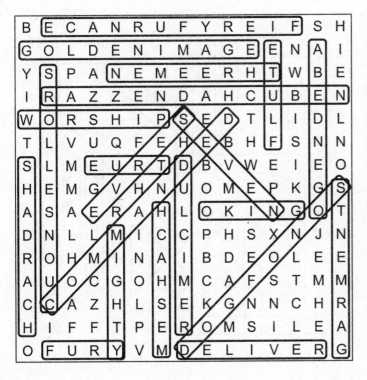

```
D A V I D R A W T U O S T R O
R E I G N I N G A D I R C K M I
O T H T Z Q X B T I O H S E H
L H E I U U Q E A R N Y G P H
E V A O S I H T N E S O H C C
H O R N W I T H O I L U E O T
T F T D Y W E L I N R N I U E
F C H I L D R E N T E G N T R
O E L Y U E O H T L F E H T N
T D K T Q S U E E J U S T O E
I W H P E W D M D E S T O N V
R H C I N R P I A S E P W A E
I I A N O I N T Y S D H E N M F
P R E L S F O E E E H G I C F
S N O S S I H F O H C T C E O
```

22

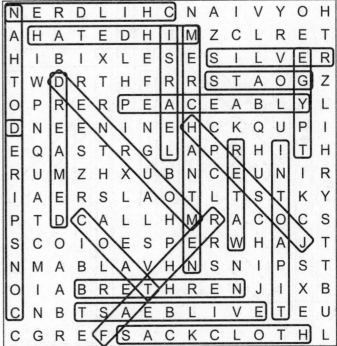

```
A K N N S D E Y O R T S E D A
T U O H S T A E R G A H S A S
P R I E S T S O P U P O W N T
M Y O F A C S H H I L U H C E
K M H W E E R S S G N T C I P
S E C C Z L O I E B L E W N M
S H O U T J L X A V I D G U
A M M O Q U G D T Q E N K O R
P L P A R N U T P Y I W H R T T
O L A R N I R S O U N S E H E
T M S D I T R E A L Y L E F L
E L S G N R B N D L M O L D E
M K E H R R O L E H T F O K R A S
A F D R Y M Y P E O P L E C Y T
C F R E
```

23

```
B E C A N R U F Y R E I F S H A
G O L D E N I M A G E E N A I
Y S P A N E M E E R H T W B E
I R A Z Z E N D A H C U B E N L
W O R S H I P S E D T L I D N
T L V U Q F E H B H F S N O
S L M E U R T D B V W E I E O
H E M G V H N U O M E P K G S
A S A E R A H L O K I N G T T
D N L L M I C C P H S X N J N
R O H M I N A I B D E O L E E
A U O C G O H M C A F S T M M
C A Z H I L S E K G N N C H R
H I F F T P E R O M S I L E A
O F U R Y V M D E L I V E R G
```

24

```
N E R D L I H C N A I V Y O H
A H A T E D H I M Z C L R E T
H I B I X L E S E S I L V E R
T W D R T H F R R S T A O G Z
O P R E R P E A C E A B L Y L
D N E E N I N E H C K Q U P I
E Q A S T R G L A P R H I H
R U M Z H X U B N C E U N I R
I A E R S L A O T L T S T K Y
P D C A L L H M R A C O C S
S C O I O E S P E R W H A J T
N M A B L A V H N S N I P S U
O I A B R E T H R E N J I X B
N B T S A E B L I V E T E U
C G R E F S A C K C L O T H L L
```

ANSWERS

25

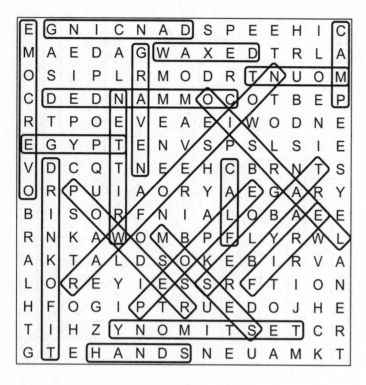

26

27

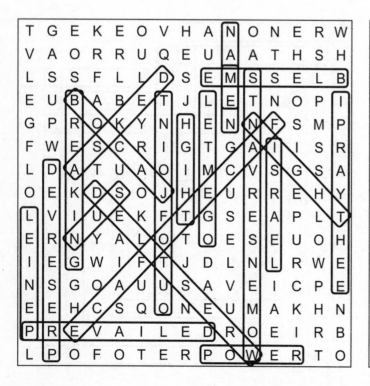

28

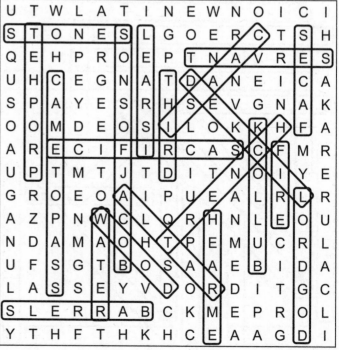

ANSWERS

29

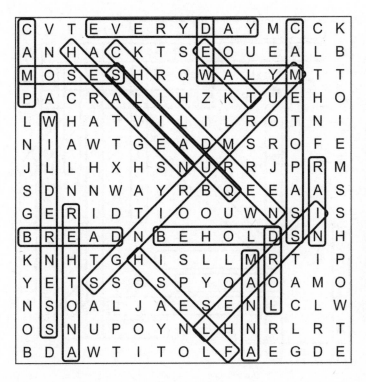

```
I N C E X P P I B K E R I O E
R I S E E O S W D G T O N N V
E A A L W O R D S R A H A B Q
O T T A I A U M E N O C Y L U
M N U G N F L A X U O I I O M
S U C H D A Y L S N B R K O M
H O T O K I E T F L E T D B
I M O N W C H X P O O J H P U
E N W I O O N S N Q U R T S
R C G N L U M J H O U S E R I
S T R D D N L E D S P Z E S N
Y H H E O T A V N Y C K D R E
Z E F O O R E A T E L R A C S
B I Y R R Y I G C K S H Y P S
W N T E S O C R H A T M S A G
```

30

```
L F W T H E R O L W L H L T C
L O C S E T I L E A R S I E I L
B S S R N M E A I T B H I V L
O Y S A M O G H J E O R O O L
H M A R N T N O T R V E A B F
F E P K E C R L C D E S S A P
D R O L S D T E C L H F L V E
R X T O A I N I P P E P N I D
Y G E N D R O O F P N A N H S
G Q M P A T E P W Y I O N A R
R U A O M P R I E S T S B R R
O H C I R E J C H S T T S V T
U R E Y C M B A E L S N H E S
N H H O A E S T L A S B E S B
D O F T H E C O V E N A N T V
```

31

```
C V T E V E R Y D A Y M C C K
A N H A C K T S E O U E A L B
M O S E S H R Q W A L Y M T T
P A C R A L I H Z K T U E H O
L W H A T V I L I L R O T N I
N I A W T G E A D M S R O F E
J L L H X H S N U R R J P R M
S D N N W A Y R B Q E E A A S
G E R I D T I O O U W N S I S
B R E A D N B E H O L D S N H
K N H T G H I S L L M R T I P
K Y E T S S O S P Y O A O A M O
I N S O A L J A E S E N L C L W
O S N U P O Y N L H N R L R T
B D A W T I T O L F A E G D E
```

32

```
A M D R O L E H T F O D R O W
L L N S S N T A C H K Y H M A
L A A S T K O N S R P S O M S
N W L O I O N D A H O C K R T
K U F H C T E F K D U Z C A E
N M C A K E S U E O A C L S D
I R P I S E U L L R O H U I N
R H L H E L O A E H Y R N D O
D N N S G I L H P S A C O B W
A R S Y E J H B A M R Q U T O
E H N K N A D A N C E S W H N
R S L T T H L R W A K H I B R
B N N H P P F R D U M A D N A
A O N G T O O E N O R O O D E
A G V E S S E L R A I N W P F
```

ANSWERS

33

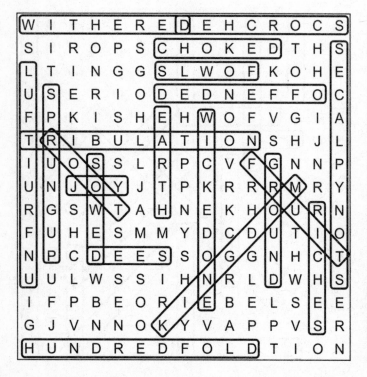

34

O T Y A P E R L L B A R A K E
N A T I R A M A S R E E S I S
U N S P I Z B V E D O N I B O
K S T R E N G T H E N O K W P
E W V L S I O L Q U K U N N X
T E O K T S W P P E M R O E V
H R T U M X L A W Y E R H W E
J E R I C H O I S L R T A S H
O D E A D E V A K M C L O T A
M N R I Z R E P R E Y O M H E
D E S E T L S H N F W D E I V
N A I V H L D C L E V I T E M
P A U U O T Y X N K L N S V L
O T S Q S G O I E P T N Z E A
O X A K T B B N N L B E A S T

35

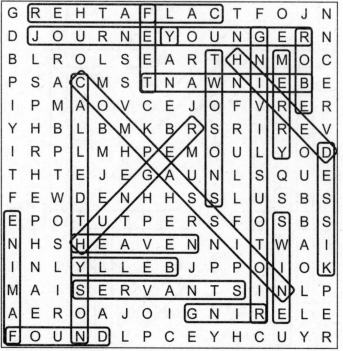

36

G R E H T A F L A C T F O J N
D J O U R N E Y O U N G E R N
B L R O L S E A R T H N M O C
P S A C M S T N A W N I E B E
I P M A O V C E J O F V R E R
Y H B L B M K B R S R I R E V
I R P L M H P E M O U L Y O D
T H T E J E G A U N L S Q U E
F E W D E N H H S S L U S B A
E P O T U T P E R S F O S B I
N H S H E A V E N N I T W A K
I M A I L Y L L E B J P P O I L P
M A I S E R V A N T S I N L P
A E R O A J O I G N I R E L E
F O U N D L P C E Y H C U Y R

ANSWERS

37

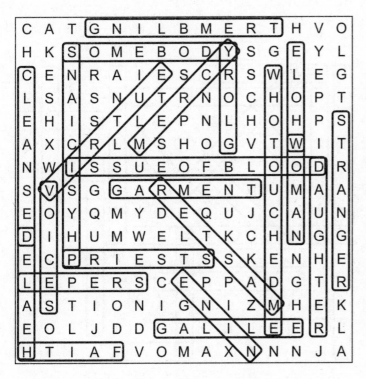

38

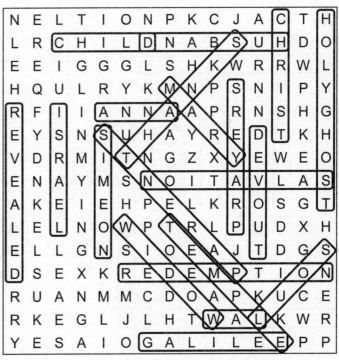

39

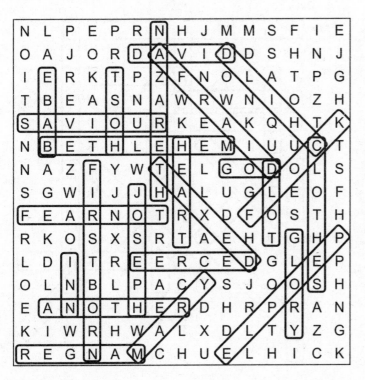

40

ANSWERS

41

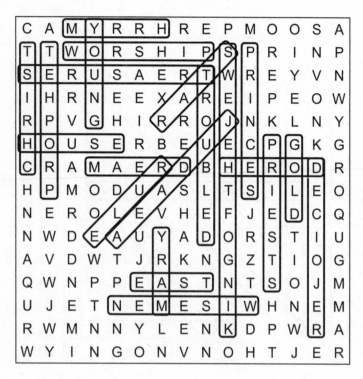

```
C A M Y R R H R E P M O O S A
T T W O R S H I P S P R I N P
S E R U S A E R T W R E Y V N
I H R N E E X A R E I P E O W
R P V G H I R R O J N K L N Y
H O U S E R B E U E C P G K G
C R A M A E R D B H E R O D R
H P M O D U A S L T S I L E O
N E R O L E V H E F J E D C Q
N W D E A U Y A D O R S T I U
A V D W T J R K N G Z T I O G
Q W N P P E A S T N T S O J M
U J E T N E M E S I W H N E M
R W M N N N Y L E N K D P W R A
W Y I N G O N V N O H T J E R
```

42

```
I P T A L I O N S H X N G P W
N E J E S S E N I S U B D L O
G T W E L V E M A R H D D J N
N P K I N S F O L K T H S E M
I A R T S P Q U L T E W E R G
D R V O E D I J C L R D J U E
N E N E Z N O H P J A P E S M
A N I L N S A M D E Z A M A D
T T W S E N E R X O A S O L E
S S A P O T E M A C N S M E V
R W H E A R T O E M P O L M S
E R E R U T A T S K E V T C H
D T P P X O F H A C U E L Z I
N A M L L K O E F L B R F R G
U B R E A N N R E H T A F A H
```

43

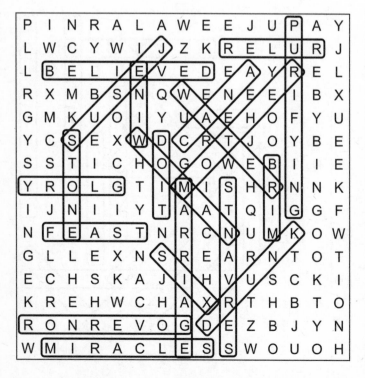

```
P I N R A L A W E E J U P A Y
L W C Y W I J Z K R E L U R J
L B E L I E V E D E A Y R E L
R X M B S N Q W E N E E I B X
G M K U O I Y U A E H O F Y U
Y C S E X W D C R T J O Y B E
S S T I C H O G O W E B I I E
Y R O L G T I M I S H R N N K
I J N I I Y T A A T Q I G G F
N F E A S T N R C N U M K O W
G L L E X N S R E A R N T O T
E C H S K A J I H V U S C K I
K R E H W C H A X R T H B T O
R O N R E V O G D E Z B J Y N
W M I R A C L E S S W O U O H
```

44

```
L M L A N D E W O L L O F O L
E S I S W R E O X E D A E P H
B J H S B P V R E T E P A B D
I R F I L L E D C R E W R R O
K E G N I H T O N E P O N L O
A O F K N G S F S S I M O N J
Y P N O O U I G W G A R T T I
T L H Z S H K O N S D M A M Y
I X O E Z T E D H M W E U E E
O A J W O A E N E M A L G L M
N M S P M Y M N L F I S H E S
P I H A A R J A P O Q U T D K
N G I R O N Y U S B S I A E C
Z A P S T O L L C O E J T E R
E K S O Y I N G K O T U N N I
```

ANSWERS

45

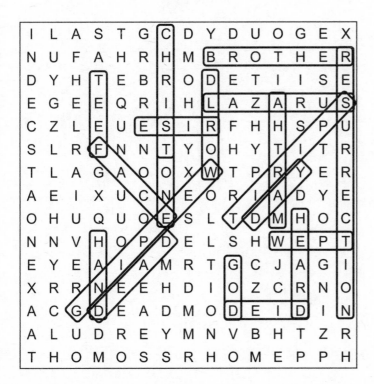

```
O Y E S U O H A L C H J E V E
R M A J N R C L I M B E D C K
G O S O N L I N T E A S A U C
C R R Y G E R Y T H D U M G H
A N I F C S T O L S W S M A N
J A E U E O X Q E D O A S U N
N R V L R U M U L A H L R T P
N E S L A F O O S A L V M E K
F N P Y I B F R R K O A U R E
A N R O J R B B O E O T R S I
R I A N U R A E O C H I E F P
E S T O E H T T P S T O D O P
N T F E P U B L I C A N S T D
M E S G O S S A L A I N G C R
H A S T E V A S E E K F E A Y
```

46

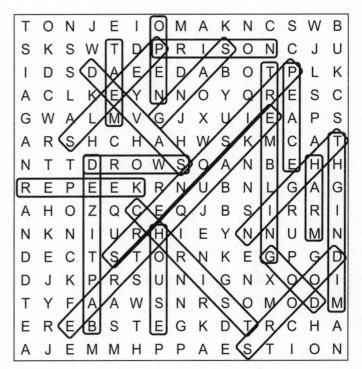

```
T O N J E I O M A K N C S W B
S K S W T D P R I S O N C J U
I D S D A E E D A B O T P L K
A C L K E Y N N O Y Q R E S C
G W A L M V G J X U I E A P S
A R S H C H A H W S K M C A T
N T T D R O W S O A N B E H H
R E P E E K R N U B N L G A I
A H O Z Q C E Q J B S I R R N
N K N I U R H I E Y N N U M N
D E C T S T O R N K E G P G D
D J K P R S U N I G N X O O I
T Y F A A W S N R S O M O D M
E R E B S T E G K D T R C H A
A J E M M H P P A E S T I O N
```

47

```
I L A S T G C D Y D U O G E X
N U F A H R H M B R O T H E R
D Y H T E B R O D E T I I S E
E G E E Q R I H L A Z A R U S
C Z L E U E S I R F H H S P U
S L R F N N T Y O H Y T I T R
T L A G A O O X W T P R Y E R
A E I X U C N E O R I A D Y E
O H U Q U O E S L T D M H O C
N N V H O P D E L S H W E P T
E Y E A I A M R T G C J A G I
X R R N E E H D I O Z C R N O
A C G D E A D M O D E I D I N
A L U D R E Y M N V B H T Z R
T H O M O S S R H O M E P P H
```

MORE GREAT LARGE PRINT PUZZLES!

Bible Memory Crosswords Large Print

Here's a collection of crosswords sure to satisfy. The "clue" for each puzzle is a memory verse, with several key words missing—you'll need to remember (or look up) those missing words to plug them into the puzzle grid.

Paperback / 978-1-63609-105-1 / $6.99

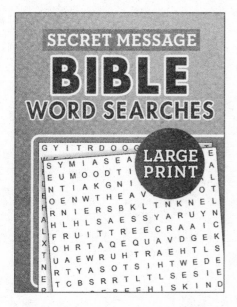

Secret Message Bible Word Searches Large Print

These large print puzzles provide a brief passage with search words highlighted. When the puzzle is solved, there's a special bonus: The leftover letters spell out a "secret message," a Bible trivia question related to the puzzle theme!

Paperback / 978-1-64352-030-8 / $6.99

Find These and More from Barbour Publishing at Your Favorite Bookstore
www.barbourbooks.com